COMMUNITY SERVICE LEARNING FOR LIFE SKILLS AND COMPETENCIES

A HANDBOOK FOR TEACHERS

Dr. Nirmala Arul & Dr. A Radhakrishnan Nair

ISBN 979-8-89026-975-1

I lovingly dedicate this Handbook,
a joyful endeavour

To

Sr. Cyril Mooney IBVM (1936-2023)

Who believed in Community Service Learning
and practised it in the Loreto schools in India and
who was my source of inspiration for undertaking to do this work

Sr. Cyril has been my inspiration. In the beginning, I was curious to know the reason why the students who studied under her care were generous, motivated and engaged whole-heartedly in civic responsibilities. I began to visit Loreto Day School, Sealdah, often, the place where she established the first Rainbow Home, in order to interact more closely with the students, staff and with her as well, to better understand the secret behind her charisma. Her purpose to instill in children the spirit of service, found resonance within me. Whatever I did and pursued subsequently, was in response to her oft-repeated words that echoed in my mind. She would tell me that children should be able to reach out to others, through education or community service and build self-esteem in the down-trodden and marginalized sections of society. This would also bring a sense of fulfilment to the students belonging to more affluent homes, enabling them to focus on giving back to society. Furthermore, this would become a life-long habit for them and bring about change in society.

The measures she adopted in those days, when awareness of social issues were few and far between, to motivate people to step out of their comfort zones and help in the upliftment of others, were far ahead of the times and transformative. She urged the students to reach beyond the classroom and engage in community service in their localities; this radical step entailed their moving out of the four walls of their homes and identifying those children who were not receiving any school education or were employed as domestic child labour or silently bore the scars of abuse, brutality and domestic violence. Through Community Service Learning, she taught the children to be aware of the reality of the world outside and empowered them to respond to the needs of society in a more organic manner.

It is the selfless work and care that she displayed through her deeds, that made a profound impact on me. Her actions motivated me to take up Community Service Learning as my PhD research topic, for which I remain indebted to her.

CONTENTS

TESTIMONIALS

I recommend this book, most enthusiastically, to the vast army of educators in our country and beyond, as a valuable 'vade mecum' that will inspire, guide and point the way.

Fr. Stephen Mavely SDB
Vice Chancellor, ADBU
Assam Don Bosco University, Guwahati, Assam - India

This handbook will be an invaluable treasure for educators who are committed to an education that brings about social change and justice in our societies. This is suitable in cross-cultural contexts and will inspire many to maintain an educational culture of human dignity in our ever-changing world. This practical tool may empower many young people to develop their personal potential and to create a better world both for themselves and their fellow human beings.

Sr. Noelle Corscadden IBVM
Former General Leader of the Institute of the Blessed Virgin Mary
Ireland

This handbook is prepared with a view of service learning from an Indian perspective and offers a thorough description of approaches to service learning as well as a detailed description of the author's own experience developing them that will surely be helpful for teachers approaching this pedagogy.

Ms. Luz Avruj
CLAYSS, Argentina

This handbook will help all those involved in school education foster a sense of one-ness where love and service of the other are valued and promoted.

Sr. Anita Braganza IBVM
Former Provincial of South Asia Province, USA

FOREWORD

It is a pleasure to write a Foreword to the Handbook on 'Community Service Learning for Life Skills and Competencies' authored by Dr. Nirmala Arul and Dr. A Radhakrishnan Nair – a work based on an outstanding doctoral thesis of the former, submitted to and defended at Don Bosco University, guided and supervised by the latter.

Dr. A Radhakrishnan Nair is considered the foremost expert and practitioner in the field of Life Skills Education. With long years of experience in various institutions of eminence behind him, he remains an untiring advocate of its efficacy in transforming the educational scenario in the country. His association with Don Bosco University as an Adjunct Faculty provided him with the opportunity to guide a number of our research scholars in the vital areas of acquiring life skills and developing competencies for a more fulfilling life.

Dr. Nirmala Arul, upon getting registered for her doctoral programme at our University, was fascinated by our community engagement programme (also known as Service-Learning Programme); and, eventually, under the guidance of Dr. A Radhakrishnan Nair, she embarked on making an alliance between his area of expertise and our concept of community engagement as a learning and formative tool in education. Her Doctoral Thesis and this book are a testimony to the value addition that this merger of ideas, concepts, and praxis has highlighted.

***** ***** *****

'Community', 'Service', 'Learning', 'Life Skills', and 'Competency Skills' – these are seamlessly interwoven concepts that have been succinctly dealt with in this Handbook, almost in the style of self-learning modules. This can be a very potent tool in the hands of teachers, empowering them to introduce 'life-skills based community service learning' in their institutions, to add a much-needed dimension in mentoring and guiding their students in their continuous search for growth – physical, mental, spiritual, and social.

Community Engagement, Community Service and Service Learning are intrinsically related to the core principles and purposes of education; but they have not, by and large, made serious inroads into institutions and their thinking today. It is hoped that wide dissemination of this book and its lucid and compelling presentations will bring about a change in that scenario.

✸✸✸✸✸ ✸✸✸✸✸ ✸✸✸✸✸

Let me end this short forward to the book with a brief summary of Don Bosco University's ongoing involvement in Service Learning allied with Community Engagement over the last several years.

From the very inception of Don Bosco University, we have been emphasizing that one of the distinctive marks of our university is its community involvement, an engagement that has earned it the distinction of being recognized as 'An Engaged University' – an involvement and engagement manifested:

- In bonding with our neighbouring communities through extension work that benefits them,

- In helping to form, in our students and faculty alike, an empathy for their (the village community's) often difficult lives,

- In facilitating reflection by our students and faculty on these engagements and experiences for their own personal growth and enrichment,

- In consultancy geared to support entrepreneurship ventures and start-ups in these communities,

- In organizing periodic skill training programmes, like Swabalamban, for the benefit of the young people in these communities and, finally, also

- In supporting and encouraging socially relevant research on these developments, experiences, and expertise.

With all these experiences in hand over a period of 10 years, we formally launched 'Service Learning' as a unique feature of our university in 2018 where:

- We introduced, for every student, modules in service-learning relevant to their own branch of study to provide them with the theory and concepts behind community engagement.

- We arranged practical engagements, internships, etc., to get to grips with everyday realities in our neighborhoods.

- We taught them to combine these academic inputs and their experiences in community service and engagements with meaningful reflection, reporting, and documentation.

- Our final goal was to reach that stage where we can certify that our students are dependable human beings - good citizens of our country and the larger world - who will undoubtedly leave footprints as involved and engaged human beings wherever they live and work.

We started with no preconceptions; we interacted with the experts; we reflected on our experiences; and we developed our own unique programme from scratch… and, step by step, we are trying to ensure that its values seep deeply into practically everything that we do in the University by way of teaching, learning, research and extension works.

***** ***** *****

I recommend this book, most enthusiastically, to the vast army of educators in our country and beyond, as a valuable 'vade mecum' that will inspire, guide and point the way.

Fr. Stephen Mavely SDB
Vice Chancellor
Assam Don Bosco University, Guwahati, Assam - India
09 March 2023

PREFACE

The purpose of writing this handbook is to share with the teaching fraternity my experience of incorporating community service learning into the school curriculum and its impact. As a teacher and as a school administrator, I have engaged the students in outreach programs for various reasons and I have always noticed that, after a series of activities, there were positive attitudinal and behavioral changes among the students. When I decided to do a Ph.D. course in the field of Education, I wanted to do something on outreach activities and find out their impacts on students. When my research guide, Dr. A. Radhakrishnan Nair asked me why I was interested in this topic, I told him that I would like the students to become good human beings. He put forward the view that parents have dreams for their children and they want their children to be placed in good positions in life. This question made me to reflect deeply and I realized that children needed life skills to reach their highest potential and become who they are capable of becoming. Further, I came across the concept of community service learning which means "Learn to Serve and Serve to Learn". Dr. Nair and myself attended a training session on how to integrate Community Service Learning in school education in CLAYSS (Centro Latinoamericano de Aprendizaje y Servicio Solidario), an institution that promotes innovative pedagogy. I understood the difference between community service and community service learning and since my focus was to teach life skills, it led me to use community service learning as a vehicle to impart life skills and develop competencies.

There are ten core life skills defined by The World Health Organization (WHO), which are essential to adjust and adapt to day-to-day life situations and that will enable students to excel in their personal as well as professional life. Life skills are taught in many different ways in schools. At times, these are taught like any other subject within classrooms and at other times these are imparted through sports, yoga, drama, music, etc. Imparting life skills through long hours of community service learning has not been explored much in Indian schools. I see there are many challenges; taking children out of the school campus is an uphill task. When I appealed to the schools to do community service learning intervention,13 schools rejected my request. A few of the reasons that they mentioned were, that they do not get enough time to complete their academic portions; it is risky to take children out of school; the parents may disapprove of their children going out; the teachers are not trained, etc.

I share this information with you, to understand so that you are aware of the difficulties in introducing community service learning and the importance of inculcating life skills among children. With the invention of Artificial Intelligence (AI), the robots/humanoid replace humans in many places for various reasons such as, the robots do not make mistakes, they do not take leave, fewer maintenance costs for them, etc. If we do not want our children to be replaced by robots, we need to impart life skills among school children so that they learn to be efficient as well as effective. I conducted 2 hours and 4 hours (including preparation and reflection) of community service learning activities with 9th-grade children based on the syllabus. In total, 120 hours of community service learning intervention activities including the preparation and reflection for 8 months of duration were conducted. A test was conducted using a standardized life skills assessment scale to measure the level of life skills of students, before and after the community service learning intervention. It was found that there was a significant positive impact on the children's life skills. Another test was conducted after 6 months, using the same scale, and it was found that the children's life skills were stable and so it has proved that structured community service learning has made a significant positive impact on life skill development among school children.

The objective of this handbook is to give a basic guidelines for the administrators of educational institutions and teachers on how to integrate community service learning into the school curriculum. The process of developing a community service learning module and the process adopted for introducing the same in selected schools were explained in a simple manner.

I hope that it will help schools to introduce community service learning keeping in mind the skills and competency development of the children, and at the same time, without compromising on the syllabus and teaching in the schools.

I take this opportunity to thank Dr. (Fr) Stephen Mavely SDB, the Vice Chancellor of Assam Don Bosco university for writing the eloquent forward for the Handbook. I feel blessed to have received comments on the Handbook from Sr. Noelle Corscadden, the former General Leader of the Institute of the Blessed Virgin Mary (IBVM), Sr. Anita Braganza IBVM, the former Provincial of South Asia Province. Fr. George Mutholi SJ, Luz Avruj from CLYASS, Sri S. M. Vijayanand, former Chief Secretary, State Government of Kerala, and Sri. Yogender Chaudhry, former Chief Income Tax Commissioner and Executive Director, Nehru Yuva Kendra Sangathan. Their kind words and appreciation inspire me to explore more on this field of study.

My special thanks to Dr. A Radhakrishnan Nair for being my Guru, his constant support and guidance. I feel privileged to have him as the coauthor of the book. My special appreciation to many school Principals, teachers of different boards, family, friends, and children (especially who were part of the intervention). I would like to express my gratitude to the present Institute and Province leadership team of the Institute of the Blessed Virgin Mary (IBVM) for their support and encouragement for this publication. Finally, I am indebted to thank Sr. Teresa McGlinchey, Mrs. Kaveri Dutt and Mrs. Nandini Bhattacharjee for doing the proof reading of the text.

Dr. Nirmala Arul IBVM

Chapter 1

INTRODUCTION

1. Education is the most critical factor that contributes to the progress of any society. School education helps in the formation of a sound personality and character-building in children. The purpose of education is learning to know, learning to do, learning to live together, and learning to be (Delors, J, 1996). According to Swami Vivekananda, education must be life-building, man-making, character-building, and assimilation of ideas. Education to him is the manifestation of perfection that a person already possesses. To Mahatma Gandhi "an all-round drawing out of the best in child and man - body, mind, and spirit" is the purpose of education.

2. As globalization has opened up vistas of opportunities to the younger generation, the traditional perspectives of education are changing and paving the way to address the needs of the global world. The conventional methods of teaching are slowly fading away, whereas new-age methods of learning are in place. The outbreak of COVID-19 has paved the way for a blended form of teaching, both online and classroom.

3. Experiential learning is gathering momentum in many schools along with innovative learning methods. As Sivalingam and Yunus (2017) stated, the combination of conventional and out-of-box approaches is of utmost importance to leading

a successful life in the 21st century. Only then students will be enabled to experience the three dimensions of education, namely the ethical and cultural, scientific and technological, and economic and social. Education is a social experience through which children learn about themselves, develop their interpersonal skills, and acquire basic knowledge and skills (McDonnell, 2017).

4. The Indian National Educational Policy 2020 states that "Education is fundamental for achieving full human potential, developing an equitable and just society, and promoting national development". It promulgates experiential and skill-based learning. It also recognizes the importance of soft skills such as communication, teamwork, problem-solving, decision-making, analytical thinking, resilience, etc. as imperative skills.

5. A school curriculum that incorporates life skills education, enhances creativity among children. Students are better able to grasp and learn new skills at an early age, and thus they become more creative, and competent. The teaching of life skills is considered one of the five features of National Education Policy (NEP) 2020. The NEP 2020 stresses the need for holistic education and asserts that, "the aim of education will not only be cognitive development but also building character and creating holistic and well-rounded individuals equipped with the key 21st century skills".

6. Ultimately, knowledge is a deep-seated treasure and education helps in its manifestation as the perfection which is already within an individual. All aspects of curriculum and pedagogy will be reoriented and revamped to attain these critical goals. Specific sets of skills and values across domains will be identified for integration and incorporation at each stage of learning, from preschool to higher education.

7. As Kay (2009), in his study, states that students need an education that offers skills to enable them to thrive in a complex, connected, and constantly changing world. When

students leave school, they must be empowered with a deeper knowledge of academic content and with 21st century skills which in turn, will help them apply their knowledge and work with others and manage their lives.

8. The basic purpose of education is to impart knowledge, attitude, and skills. While knowledge is imparted through classroom learning sessions, attitudes, and skills are ignored. According to Yuen, et al (2010), appropriate skills and attitudes are necessary for competence and successful careers of students. By introducing life skills in all areas of school education, students will have academic engagement, belonging, discipline, fairness, linking the school with the community, student voices, extra-curricular activities, peer relations, safety, and teacher support and will help develop appropriate attitudes and skills in children.

9. In this scenario, it is more important to teach our children at school the power of interdependence and empathy than transmitting educational content that leads them to get higher academic results and admission into prestigious professional colleges. Today, to live in harmony and integrity, what one needs is a greater sense of self-awareness, empathy, communication, and interpersonal relationship skills (Gogoi et al., 2015).

10. Life skills taught in schools when they are young can affect healthy signs of growth in one's personality. It is this which will invariably enhance our education system to produce effective fruits in one's life and living (Balda and Sangwan, 2015). Life skills classes will have a greater and lasting effect on the students. There are many ways to teach life skills in schools, like introducing it as a part of the curricular activity or co-curricular sessions or by conducting training programmes in life skills (Ranjan and Nair, 2015).

11. It has been proved that children do learn quickly when they are exposed to an experiential way of learning (Powell and Wells, 2010) and community service learning could be one of the ways to impart life skills to children. Service learning

has a pedagogical linkage in which educators and students learn together from experience and engage together in the transformation of reality. It implies action and reflection on the practice and the establishment of solidarity links that allow one to act and learn from the community.

12. This handbook will explain how life skills and competence could be enhanced in school children by involving them in community service learning.

Chapter 2

COMMUNITY SERVICE LEARNING

2.1   Community Service

Community service is work done by a person or group of people that benefits others. People do not get paid to perform community service.

- It is often organized through a local place of worship, a school, or a non-profit organization. It is voluntary work that is completed for free in a given community with no expectation or regard for money from the beneficiary. This may include one activity or a series of activities from one person or multiple persons.

- Community Service is designed to improve the quality of life for community residents, to solve particular problems related to their needs, including areas such as health care, child care, literacy training, educational welfare, social services, transportation, housing, and neighborhood improvement, public safety, disaster relief, crime prevention and control, recreation, rural development, community development, among others.

- It can help any group of people in need: children, senior citizens, and people who are differently abled. It could also involve the care for animals; improve the environment in places like local parks, historical places, and scientific areas.

- Community service programmes may be mandatory or voluntary and these are planned for students to perform acts of service that are beneficial to the community.

- Community service does not have a particular curriculum designed for it. It is not integrated within existing school or classroom curriculum nor does it have classroom objectives.

- Community service is termed as an activity that provides benefits to the recipient and addresses social issues like recycling, homelessness, and the environment. It often takes place after school hours and is not formally related to any academic course (Furco, 1996).

- The elements of community service are that the work done is unpaid and the community is benefited. It is considered to be a way for students to help others by volunteering their time, effort, or talents, and is performed to benefit others without any compensation in whatsoever form (Camara, 2012).

- This innovative approach encourages students to develop an awareness and understanding of civic responsibility and of the role they can play in supporting and strengthening their communities. Individual development and social development can flourish for students who are involved in community service (Farahmandpour, 2011).

- The impact of community service on the students depends on the efficacy of the programme. It is a meaningful experience that teaches the young to realize the power of human potential to create change and gives space to explore reality, ask questions, reflect, and act (Herzberg, 2006).

- Community service helps the student not only to become autonomous individuals but also members of a larger community to which they are accountable. It instills in youth an ethic of civic responsibility, seen as an instrument for processing civic change (Bonnet, 2008).

2.2 Community Service Learning

In the 21st century, students must learn to link what they have learned in academic courses to real-life situations in the work environment. Community service learning provides an opportunity to students with meaningful opportunities to make connections between what they study in the classroom with the real world to practise it. Robinson and Torres (2015) also suggest that community service learning provides students with opportunities to apply what they are learning in the classroom to solve real-life problems in real-world contexts.

- Community service learning is a structured learning experience that combines community service with classroom instruction, focusing on explicit learning objectives, preparation, reflection, and civic responsibility.

- Community service learning projects are developed, implemented, and evaluated in collaboration with the stakeholders i.e. the community, school, students, and teachers.

- Professor Freddy Cardoza defined community service learning as a 'Pedagogy' (or a specific teaching-learning approach) that has few lectures, and its more interactive hands-on educational strategy provides students with instruction while leading them through a meaningful community service process.

- The Canadian Alliance for community service learning articulated its first definition in 2006, as an educational approach that integrates service in the community with intentional learning activities. Both educational institutions and community organizations work together towards outcomes that are mutually beneficial.

- The National Service Learning Clearing House (2012) defines service-learning as "a teaching and learning strategy that integrates meaningful community service with instruction and reflection to enrich the learning experience, teach civic responsibility and strengthen communities".

- In community service learning, students:

  a) participate in an organized service activity that meets identified community needs, and

  b) reflect on the service activity in such a way as to gain a future understanding of course content, a broader appreciation of the discipline, and an enhanced sense of personal values and civic responsibility (Camara, 2012, p.11).

- Community service learning integrates classroom teaching with reflection and useful service to the community. It aims at the application of academic skills and knowledge to address a community need, issue, or problem and to enhance student learning.

- Corporation for National Community Service, (1990) has identified two components in community service learning, viz.

  a) The method under which students learn and develop through active participation in community service learning, and

  b) Thoughtfully organizes service experiences that meet actual community needs that (are) integrated into the student's academic curriculum or provide structured time (for reflection), and that enhances what is taught in school by extending student learning beyond the classroom and into the community.

- A community service learning programme involves students in activities that address community-identified needs while developing, polishing, and honing their academic skills and commitment to their community.

- Service learning is a teaching strategy that invites students to identify, research, and address real community challenges and issues using knowledge and skills learned in the classroom. Service learning takes place in structured time to investigate community needs, thoughtful planning of the service project, and guided reflection on their service experience (Kasinath, 2013).

- Community service learning is a teaching method that utilizes what is taught in a classroom and equips the student to apply this knowledge, in real-world situations. It is designed to make classroom learning meaningful and relevant, to help students apply their learning beyond the school setting. The integration of service experiences into the curriculum as an instructional strategy that can be used as an in-class experience and as an extracurricular activity.

- According to Keen and Hall, (2009) community service learning becomes a way for students to learn basic skills, and enable them to apply what they learn in the class. It is planned around students' learning and active participation rather than teaching. A focus on efficiently and effectively addressing needs with the community, and not just for the community. This experience actively involves the students in all stages, from planning to assessment.

- Community service becomes community service learning when there is a deliberate and explicit connection made between services and learning opportunities which are accompanied by reflection and evaluation.

- Community service learning challenges students to become active participants in their community. It enables them to discover the connections between academic objectives and the service experience. Community service learning intends to develop the community through valuable and meaningful service projects (Todd, 2008).

- Community service learning evolved as a vehicle to strengthen students' learning, reconnect them with their communities, counter the imbalance between learning and living, and repair the broken connection between learning and community. Students learn to serve and serve to learn through active reflection during community service learning.

2.3 Historical Evolution of Community Service Learning Around the Globe and in India

1. Ignatian Pedagogical Paradigm (IPP) is rooted in the spiritual exercises devised in the 16th century by Ignatius of Loyola, the founder of the Society of Jesus (commonly known as Jesuits). The five elements of IPP i.e., context, experience, reflection, action, and evaluation remain a statement of educational operating methods and objectives. Chubbuck S, M (2007) explains that this method of education focuses on knowing the context of the students, involving them in experiential learning by engaging the students in various experiences, and build opportunities for reflection which help them to think about what they have learned, what it means to them and feel the need for action, and lastly assess them on the specific areas of growth.

2. John Bosco was born in 1815, popularly known as Don Bosco, in Turin, Italy; he was a Catholic priest, educator, and writer of the 19th century. He developed teaching methods based on love rather than punishment, a method known as the Salesian preventive system. His spirit of service is alive even today among the many institutions which were established and are run by Salesian fathers. Still, community service learning pedagogy is followed by the Don Bosco educational institutions.

3. Paulo Freire was a Brazilian educator and philosopher and a leading advocate of critical pedagogy. As one of the most important critical educators of the twentieth century, Paulo Freire emphasized that education should liberate the oppressed and give freedom, especially to the marginalized and the disadvantaged. He criticized the system of education,

where students are treated like empty vessels to be filled in with knowledge. He argues that pedagogy should instead treat the learner as a co-creator of knowledge (Braa and Callero, 2006). Community service learning also evolved more strongly, based on this concept wherein, a new way of education system was introduced and the student's participation was emphasized. More importance was given to the upliftment of the deprived and the needy in society.

4. The intellectual foundation of community service learning in the United States can be traced back to the early 1900s with the work of John Dewey who promoted models of "learning by doing," and linked service to personal and social development. Unlike traditional educators who stressed rote learning and an authoritative teacher, Dewey emphasized the concept of learning by doing. John Dewey was one of the first persons to develop service-based learning in an educational setting by combining experiential learning and service to the community. The same concept was reinforced in the 1980s, by David Kolb, who developed his "Experiential Model Learning" (Kolb, 1984) which is based on Dewey's work.

5. CLAYSS (Centro Latinoamericano de Aprendizaje y Servicio Solidario) is an institution that promotes innovative pedagogy that was founded in 2002 in the Latin American Centre for Service Learning (CLAYSS). In the early 2000s, the Latin American Center for Service-Learning (CLAYSS) emphasized various points to promote its service-learning model in Latin America, Africa, and Eastern Asia as well as in Spain and Italy. CLAYSS has defined three characteristics of a service-learning project[1]:

    a. Solidarity service actions intended to meet the real and sincere needs of a community and not only for it;

---

[1] https://www.clayss.org.ar/04_publicaciones/SSLintheArts_english.pdf accessed on 26-4-2023.

b. Actions in which students have an active role from planning to the assessment stage; and

c. Actions intentionally connected with learning content and research.

To CLAYSS the key is the intentional articulation of solidarity practises with curricular knowledge. With this, the community needs, as well as the learning requirements of students, can be realized. According to their pedagogy, there are four elements in the process of service-learning projects such as, motivation, diagnosis, project designing, planning, closure, and multiplication. The mission of CLAYSS is to construct a more democratic, just, and equal approach in society (CLAYSS, 2019).

6. Campus Compact was founded in 1985 to develop service learning in colleges and universities nationwide. In 1990 the U.S. Congress passed the National and Community Service Act as a way to enhance national and community service. Therefore, community service is an integral part of social life in the US. At present, there are many countries such as Canada, Finland, Ireland, and Australia that have adapted community service learning as part of their school curriculum. The term service learning was coined in 1976 but has its roots dating back to the 1900s when educator Arthur Dunn incorporated service in the community as part of the social studies curriculum.

7. UNESCO's (2021) report "Reimagining Our Futures Together: A New Social Contract for Education" discusses the need for service learning. It highlights the need for "a new social contract for education to repair injustices while transforming the future and draw lines for the nations to follow in the years to come." The report points out that "A new social contract for education must reinforce education as a public endeavour, shared social commitment, as one of the most important human rights, and as one of the most important responsibilities of states and citizens. In turn,

one of the key roles of education is to educate citizens who advance human rights. This entails building the capabilities that make students autonomous and ethical thinkers and doers. It means equipping them to collaborate with others and developing their agency, responsibility, empathy, critical and creative thinking, alongside a full range of social and emotional skills." (UNESCO, 2021 p 47). For a new social contract for education, UNESCO openly mentions service learning as one of the main innovations in education that educators around the world should be using. It says, "Service learning and community engagement soften the walls between classroom and community, challenge students' assumptions, and connect them with broader systems, processes, and experiences beyond their own experiences." It further adds that "Community-engaged pedagogies and service learning can imbue learning with a strong sense of purpose when undertaken in a humble posture of learning. A significant reworking of the organization of schooling is necessary to fully enable pedagogies like these to advance students' abilities to undertake joint work and expand our capacities for collective deliberation and action in a spirit of solidarity" (P-52). The report further argues the importance of service learning by stating that, "The lesson must give way to pedagogies that value a diversity of methods and modalities of study and learning. There are many other ways to bring people together in common endeavours using diverse modalities of study and learning that leverage intergenerational and intercultural exchange and capitalize on the high-level abilities and knowledge of teachers. For example, problem-based and project-based educational approaches can be more participatory and collaborative than conventional lessons offer. Inquiry-based and action-research pedagogies can engage students in acquiring, applying, and generating knowledge simultaneously". (P-99)

8. The Gurukul education system that was prevalent in the Vedic period until the introduction of the English education system in India is one of the traditional forms of community

service learning. The students stayed with the "Guru" – the teacher and learned from him. The *Shishya* – the student, in turn, helped the Guru in his everyday life and participated in his community service activities. It is the oldest form of experiential learning. The education predominant at that time was holistic in nature, in which the child is considered a whole being with *panchakoshas* or five sheaths. The layers are *annamaya kosha* (physical layer), *pranamaya kosha* (life force energy layer), *manomaya kosha* (mind layer), *vijnanamaya kosha* (intellectual layer), and *anandamaya kosha* (inner self). Each layer exhibits certain distinct characteristics for the holistic development of a child taking into account the nurturing and nourishment of these five layers. The National Curriculum Framework (NCF) for ECCE (Early Childhood Care Education) 2022 has narrated it succinctly as follows[2]:

- Physical Development (*Sharirik Vikas*): Age-specific, balanced physical development, physical fitness, flexibility, strength, and endurance; development of senses; nutrition, hygiene, personal health, expansion of physical abilities; building body and habits keeping in mind one hundred years of healthy living in a human being.

- Development of Life Energy (*Pranik Vikas*): Balance and retention of energy, positive energy, and enthusiasm, smooth functioning of all major systems (digestive, respiratory, circulatory, and nervous systems) by activation of the sympathetic and parasympathetic nervous system.

- Emotional/Mental Development (*Manasik Vikas*): Concentration, peace, will and will power, courage, handling negative emotions, developing virtues (*maulyavardhan*), the will to attach and detach from work, people and situations, happiness, visual and performing arts, culture, and literature.

---

[2] NCERT (2022). National Curriculum Framework for Foundational Stage 2022. P 19-20.

- Intellectual Development (*Bauddhik Vikas*): Observation, experimentation, analytical ability, abstract and divergent thinking, synthesis, logical reasoning, linguistic skills, imagination, creativity, power of discrimination, generalization, and abstraction.

- Spiritual Development (*Chaitsik Vikas*): Happiness, love, compassion, spontaneity, freedom, aesthetic sense, and the journey of 'turning the awareness inwards.'

Panchakosha is an ancient explication of the importance of the body-mind complex in human experience and understanding. This non-dichotomous approach to human development gives clear pathways and direction toward a more holistic education. This was practiced in the ancient Indian education system through the service learning process.

9. Later, Mahatma Gandhi's schemes to uplift the deprived and the marginalized, during the freedom movement, with the tool of non-violence were indeed the beginning of community service learning in the modern era. For instance, the Harijan Sevak Sangh, the Khadi movement, and the Sarvodaya were all glimpses of community service learning started by Gandhiji during the freedom movement in India. The two core principles which stand out in Gandhian educational philosophy are vocational education and community service. Mahatma Gandhi's concept of education, *Nai Talim* (basic education), is not designed only for the development of cognitive skills, but holistic development centered around the learning and practise of a craft, and hence is also called craft-centered education. But later, the education plans failed to carry out these ideas into the new education system. The Viswa Bharati University, started by Rabindranath Tagore, had embedded the concept of community service in the curriculum. The Sriniketan project initiated by him, for the upliftment of the downtrodden people and making them self-sustainable, was another example of a community service initiative in India.

10. Community and social service were given the utmost importance in Gandhiji's scheme of *Nai Talim*. The C. D. Deshmukh Committee (1956) recommended compulsory national service for all adolescents before they could have access to higher education or employment in government. The Education Commission (1964-66) also recommended that community and social service should be an integral part of the educational process. NSS (National Service Scheme) was launched in the year 1969 while celebrating Mahatma Gandhi's Birth Centenary. The NSS aims at developing the student's personality through community service. It is offered in schools at higher secondary levels, universities, and colleges. But NSS is not open to all students in the educational institutions.

2.4 Philosophical Underpinning of Community Service Learning

1. The idea of the Ignatian Pedagogical Paradigm, John Dewey and Paulo Freire, articulate the philosophy behind community service learning. All their principles dealt with the two key relationships, namely action to reflection, and individual to society.

2. Ignatian pedagogy uses this dynamic five-step method: context, experience, reflection, action, and evaluation, along with an Ignatian vision of the human and the world to accompany the learners in their journey of growth and development. It is all about developing and questioning one's own conscience, as well as making sound and conscientious decisions (Meirose, 2001). For Jesuits, education does not only mean to live authentically enough in the world but to participate in the transformation of the world (McAvoy, 2013). The goal of Jesuit education is to produce men and women for whom discernment is a habit and a way of life (Haynes, 2007).

3. In Dewey's writings on pragmatic philosophy, progressive education has been invoked to the theory and practice of active, experiential, and student-centered learning. Dewey applied both philosophical and psychological perspectives to build his theory of education (McDermott, 1981). It is applied from elementary school to college and from project-based learning to internship programmes and also in the ongoing process of constructing a philosophical and theoretical framework for community service learning. John Dewey has been considered as the founding father of community service learning. Dewey's philosophy is both a pioneer and exemplar for the theory and practice of community service learning (Giles and Eyler, 1994).

4. Paulo Freire began his work in 1947 with adult illiterates in North-East Brazil and gradually evolved a method of work with which the word conscientization has been associated. Paulo Freire's philosophy of education was praxis of action and reflection. He vehemently believed that it is not enough for people to come together in dialogue in order to gain knowledge of their social reality. Rather, they must act together upon their environment in order to critically reflect upon their reality and so transform it through future action and critical reflection (Saleh, 2013). Freirean pedagogy is considered participatory, situated (in student thought and language), critical, democratic, dialogical, de-socializing, multi-cultural, research-oriented, activist, and effective. Freire's understanding of the relation of knowledge to action suggests learning situations that are collaborative, active, community-oriented, and grounded in the culture of the student.

5. Mahatma Gandhi advocated for a form of education that encouraged community service and character-building. Gandhi wrote: "Studies should be undertaken only with the aim of equipping oneself for service." Throughout his life, his struggle was focused on humanity. Gandhi attempted to establish certain moral and spiritual values like truth,

non-violence, non-discrimination, social justice, and self-reliance through constructive programmes. Gandhian principles are based on a set of philosophical beliefs – cooperation over competition, interdependence over rugged individualism, compassion for others over the pursuit of self-interest, and social justice over an individual's greed and achievements. The quintessence of Gandhian ethics is the well-being of all (Sarvodaya), and justice for all (Satyagraha). The Gandhian concept of social development is based on the foundation of truthfulness, love for all, harmonious relations, and service to others (Dundar, et al 2016). The philosophy of Mahatma Gandhi on community service learning can be understood from his quote "the service lies in serving others".

6. CLAYSS (2015) philosophy of community service learning emphasizes that in service learning, knowledge is used to improve something in the community and service becomes a learning experience that provides knowledge and values. Service learning becomes interwoven in a win-win relationship. Children gain new knowledge, explore new topics, and develop skills for life, work, and civic participation. It is a way of thinking about education and teaching using the corresponding teaching tools and strategies that require students to learn and develop through active participation in service activities to achieve the objectives of learning defined by the educational institution and the community.

2.5 Theoretical Underpinning of Community Service Learning

Community service learning pedagogy has been enriched with theory and practice, and it has been influenced by various theories. Community service learning evolved as a vehicle to strengthen students' learning, reconnect them with their communities, counter the imbalance between learning and living, and repair the broken connection between learning and community.

Experiential Learning theory

Community service learning literature embraces Dewey's idea that effective learning requires contextualization through application and experience. He is seen as a key contributor to community service learning theory because of his pragmatic philosophy and education as a social phenomenon that serves to reinforce the aims and methods of the society. It lays emphasis on democratic participation and student-centered educational theory (Fredericksen, 2000; Hugg and Wurdinger, 2007, Deans, 1999). John Dewey expanded a theory on education which was known as learning by doing. He believed that the knowledge learned in schools must be applied to the "real world" for the advancement of the students and the betterment of society (Dewey, 1916). Learning by doing is an effective way of learning because it helps the brain create pathways that make it easier and quicker to retain (Anzai and Simon, 1979). The students apply the theoretical knowledge to solve the problems of the community, while they practise the abstract content they learned, to understand the concept.

Social psychologist, David Kolb, considered experiential education as a process where knowledge is created through the transformation of experience. Experiential learning is an engaged learning process whereby students "learn by doing" and by reflecting on experience. It is the process of learning through experience, and is more specifically defined as 'learning through reflection on doing'. Experiential learning theory proceeds from a different set of assumptions. Ideas are not fixed but formed and re-formed through experience. Kolb's theory is linked to community service learning as a learning approach that requires both action and reflection (Chambers, 2009; Kolb, 1984).

Trial-and-Error Theory

Edward Thorndike was the initiator of the trial-and-error theory. According to Thorndike, learning takes place by trial and error. There is no readymade solution available to the problem. It is all about trying one method and observing if it works; otherwise, try another method till the problem is solved. It is an attempt to learn/solve problems by trying alternative possibilities until the correct solution or desired outcome is achieved. It leads to repeating the performance of the correct response and strengthening the association between the behaviour and its outcome. Once the behaviour is learned it is usually performed quickly with fewer errors. In community service learning, the students try to solve the problem of the community by using certain methods, and after the completion of the project, it is evaluated. If they find out that their endeavour did not work, the students try another method.

Constructivism

Constructivism is not a specific pedagogy. Piaget's theory of constructivist learning has had a wide-ranging impact on learning theories and teaching methods in education. Piaget's theory of constructivism argues that people produce knowledge and form meaning, based upon their experiences. Constructivism theory encourages students to explore an aspect of something that they have not tried or thought about, before. It covers learning theories and teaching methods. A student assimilates when he incorporates new experiences into old experiences.

Freire's Liberation Theory

Brazilian educator Paulo Freire's ideas about liberatory education have provided a theoretical anchor for several community service learning programmes and courses. Freire advocated learning situations that are collaborative, active, community-oriented, and grounded in the culture of the student (Chambers, 2009; Chovanec et al. 2012; Kajner et al., 2013). Liberation pedagogy intends to transform oppressive structures, people who are marginalised and humanized need to engage in learning and take them from where they are, by knowing the context of the social, economic, and political situation of their background. He outlined the widely influential theory of education in the pedagogy of the oppressed in 1968. His principles of education were social change, transformation, reflection, and action (Stetsenko, 2008; Deans, 1999) which is the basis of community service learning.

2.6 Community Service Learning as Pedagogy

Community service learning is aligned with the academic curriculum, with the objectives and clear goals of ensuring learning for the students. Students' academic engagement performance is good when the service and learning are connected. Students apply what they have learned in the classroom. Community service learning has a positive influence on the participants who benefit socially and academically (Ceclio et al 2011). It is a pedagogical method that connects academic content to service and connects the learning from the service experience to the content gained. It is a fertile ground to practise the abstract concept of the text (Lena, 1995). Service becomes another text for the course of study as the student participant integrates the learning with academic content. Community service learning is a teaching pedagogy because it proposes that learning takes place in and from the community. It empowers the students to become responsible learners (Schulteis, 2013). Community service learning pedagogy programme promotes comprehensive, inclusive and quality education. It meets the needs of a community. The students are involved in the planning, development, and assessment of the project. It integrates the learning content (theory) with community service. Community service learning fosters civic engagement, inclusivity, builds networks and modifies common perceptions.

Figure 2.1 explains how one could use academic knowledge to serve the community and in turn from the community service to academic learning, how one could enhance his/her knowledge and this chain of learning takes place constantly.

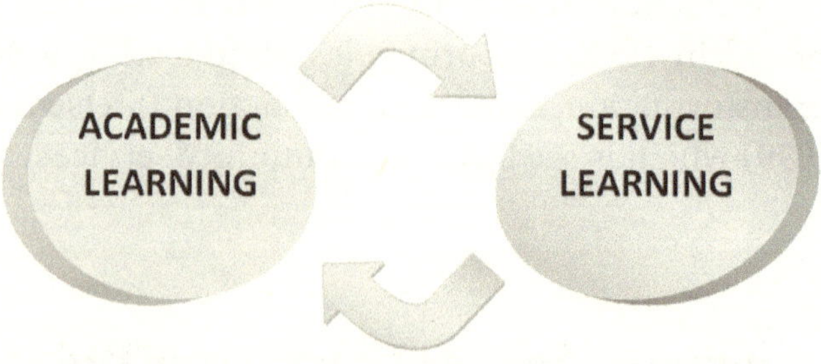

Figure: 2:1 *Academic learning and service learning (Source: Self)*

2.7 Models of Community Service Learning

a) **The Philanthropic Model** is based on the perceived need for charity. Philanthropy is all about the love of humankind. The philanthropic model is a tool where the service is done with love and care. It is best applied in cases and situations where immediate relief is required. One little act can make a lot of difference. It is about giving time, talent and reassurance for the common good. It is a collective action for the private good. The intention here is not to gather new learning, but of an immediate response to give relief to people in distress. New experiences and knowledge are an offshoot of philanthropic work.

b) **The Civic Engagement model** is all about equal participation and the voice of all citizens which democracy demands. Civic engagement has a long-term positive impact on communities, as faculty and students serve as agents of social change consistent with democratic principles. The civic engagement model renews and alters the focus of higher education institutions on service as the focal point of their mission of teaching, research, and professional service. In this approach, people actually will have to become active agents of change and not remain as mere passive recipients.

c) **The Communitarian Model** assumes that humans are social beings who see their main concern in politics as protecting their liberty and property instead of being self-interested individual egotists. Community service learning is central to developing a sense of human community at the local level. It is about civic action which becomes a public action and public action converts to collective action. The communitarian paradigm strives to characterize a good society as one, that nourishes both social virtues and individual rights.

d) **Ignatian Pedagogical Paradigm** consists of context, experience, action, reflection, and evaluation. It is used in Jesuit education around the world. Community service learning drew inspiration from the model developed by Ignatius of Loyola. The context of learning of the student includes: the real context of his/her life, the socio-economic, political and cultural context, ethos and climate of the society and the concepts that the students have already acquired. One needs to know the context of the students, the predisposition of the learner, and whether the student would benefit from personal care and concern. In terms of experience, the students get a feel or a hold on the subject, knowing facts, concepts, and principles with regard to the discipline. When the students understand the subject accurately, then they can appreciate the dynamics involved in it. The experience with the subject motivates the students. The students are exposed to participate in various intellectual activities such as analysis, comparison, synthesis, contrast, and evaluation. The students are encouraged to reflect on their experiences and come up with action-oriented projects in the service of humanity which are then evaluated.

e) **CLAYSS Model:** There are five elements in the CLAYSS service-learning framework which include motivation, diagnosis, project design, and planning, implementation and closure, and multiplication. It would be the stages of what CLAYSS calls the itinerary, a tool for planning and implementing a service learning project. The concept of service learning and its purpose are introduced to school management, teachers, students, community members, and other agencies. They are motivated and invited to be a part of the service-learning programme. Community service learning experiences are planned by students and teachers together with the community, including information about the community, their role as a service provider, and best practises for working in collaboration with community members. The participants identify the needs, and problems of the community and find out the challenges and the possibilities related to executing the activity. Once the needs of the community are found, the process of planning and preparation starts to solve the problem and the students are guided to connect their book knowledge with the real-world problem. After the planning of the activities, they are impelled to put their plan into action. All these activities are carried out in a team and in consultation with the community. Reflection is followed after every activity which helps the students to become aware of their personal learning which then is followed by closure and multiplication. The projects are evaluated with their peers and with the community and the students are encouraged to share their experiences with others.

f) **IPARD Framework** represents the student-centered inquiry model in community service learning projects. This form of community service learning framework has five stages namely investigation, planning and preparation, action, reflection, and demonstration. The students investigate the needs and problems of the community. They prepare and plan realistic and meaningful service projects and implement the plan through a direct or indirect community service learning approach. The participants make the connection between learning and action and involve others to complete every step together to get the most out of the experience.

2.8 Characteristics and Concerns of Community Service Learning

a. Community service learning links academic content and it is reciprocal in nature, benefiting both the community and the service providers by combining the service experience with a learning experience (Metcalf, 2010). It can be used in any subject area as it is an appropriate learning goal and works at all ages, especially among children. It gives sufficient time for students to reflect. It is an opportunity to use skills and knowledge in real-life situations and to extend learning beyond the classroom. It fosters a sense of caring for others (Carson and Domangue, 2012).

b. Community service learning is positive, meaningful, and real to the participants, involves cooperation rather than competitive experiences and thus promotes life skills associated with teamwork and community involvement (Hebert and Hau 2015). It offers opportunities to engage in problem-solving from which the participants gain knowledge from experience rather than only to draw abstract knowledge such as it might come from a textbook (Brown, 2011). As a result, community service learning offers powerful opportunities to acquire the habits of critical thinking i.e., the ability to identify the most important questions or issues within a real-world situation. It promotes deeper learning because the results are immediate and it is a life time experience.

c. Community service learning applies to all curriculum and students of all ages and backgrounds. It is fundamental to the teaching-learning process in and out of the classroom. It helps faculty to become better teachers, personalizes learning, and stresses the social dimension of both teaching and learning (Bringle and Hatcher, 2000; Chessin, Moore, and Theobald, 2011). When the heart is touched by direct experience, the mind may be challenged to change. It creates opportunities to be personally involved with people who are innocently suffering unjust structures, and to become a catalyst for solidarity which gives rise to intellectual inquiry and moral reflection.

d. The major concern is for the administrators of the school to understand the importance of introducing it, as a part of the school curriculum. There is an immense pressure to complete the syllabus rather than involving children in other extracurricular activities. There is a trepidation about taking children for outdoor learning as there is a fear of children's safety. The administrators of the schools may find it time consuming as there is a lot of planning and organizing involved. The challenge for the faculty is to find ways to integrate community service learning to the subjects one teaches and the project topics as it needs to be adapted and applied to their own specific situations.

2.9 Impact of Community Service Learning on Individuals and Society

Various studies have highlighted the impact of community service learning and the benefit of it to the students who are participating in the activity and to the society. A few findings are summarized below:

• High school students who participated in high-quality community service learning programmes were more likely to develop bonds with more adults; they could learn from and work with the elderly and disabled, and feel that they could trust others, besides parents and teachers to whom they could turn for help. They were able to trust and be trusted by others, be reliable and accept responsibility (Morgan and Streb, 2001).

• Students who engaged in quality community service learning programmes reported greater acceptance of cultural diversity and showed greater empathy and cognitive complexity than comparable groups. Students who engaged in community service learning were more likely to treat each other kindly, help each other, and care about giving their best (Reinders & Yourniss, J. 2009).

- In their awareness of cultural differences and attitudes, they enjoy helping others with projects, they become more interdependent and feel more comfortable communicating with ethnically diverse groups (Borden, 2007; Gutheil, Chernesky and Sherratt, 2006).

- Community service learning has a positive effect on students' interpersonal development and the ability to relate to culturally diverse groups (Conrad and Hedin, 1982).

- Middle and high school students who participated in community service learning programmes increased their grade points and test scores in reading/language, arts, and mathematics and were less likely to drop out of school. They showed an increase in measures of personal and social responsibility, competence, communication skills, and sense of educational competence (Giles and Eyler, 1994).

- Community service learning has a positive effect on the personal development of school youth. The benefits of community service learning on young people are vast, touching on almost every facet - moral, cognizant, social, and psychological development (Boss, 1994).

- They begin to ask a question, reflect, doubt, and adapt. It is an educative experience for the student. Students dealing with social problems begin to develop critical thinking (Larkin and Mahoney, 2006).

- It allows the students to solidify concepts taught in the classroom, apply their learning and discover how they can strengthen communities and positively impact society through their actions. In this process of learning, the students study many subjects in class and when they are involved in doing different action-oriented projects on various subjects, their learning becomes practical (Rhodes and Davis, 2001).

- Students understand the text better and contextualize the theory to the local needs and problems. It increases academic learning and the ability to apply what they have learned in the real world (Warren, 2012).

- They get opportunities to practise leadership quality and become resourceful and take initiative not only in their school but also in other personal, academic, and professional pursuits. Students have optimal opportunities to practise and apply content and concepts and to reflect and evaluate both their own development and the impact of their service on the local and global community. Middle school male students reported an increase in their confidence level and the ability to discern and self-esteem, self-efficacy, fewer behavioral problems, and less likely to engage in "risk" behaviors (Simons and Cleary, 2006).

- Students who engaged in community service learning experienced a structured health curriculum, and were less likely to engage in unprotected sexual activity or violent behavior.

- Students have the opportunity to do what they are learning in class through experiential education. They have a deeper understanding of themselves and their involvement in the society. They become more aware of the issues in the community and develop a sense of civic responsibility to address those issues and plan for future involvement (Astin and Sax, 1998; Skinner and Chapman, 1999).

- Students participating in community service learning, build character, gain civic responsibility, and open doors for career possibilities (Conway, Amel and Gerwien, 2009) and high school students who engage in quality community service learning programmes reported powerful impacts on both individual and society (Perry and Katula, 2001).

- In the course of community service learning, there will be community development and people will have attitudinal change towards the youth and their capacity. There will be a connection between schools and the community (Enfield and Collins, 2008).

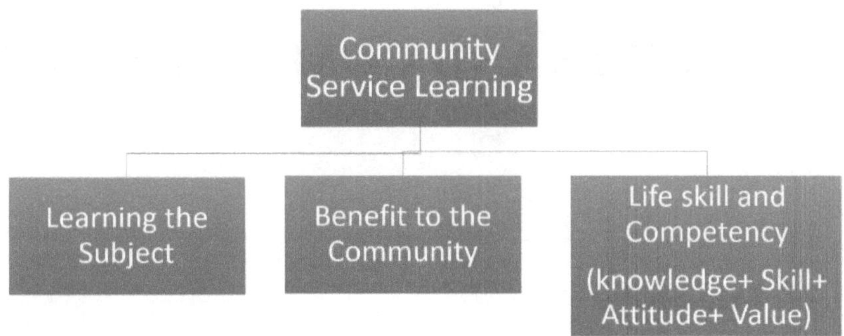

Figure 2.2: *The impact of community service learning (Source: Self)*

Since community service learning is connected to the school curriculum, the students learn the subject matter and the concepts become clearer to them as they apply the theory and put it into action. In the course of implementing the service activity, the community also benefits from the service and becomes empowered. Besides the strengthening of theoretical knowledge, the students' life skills level, and competency increase. Competency is a combination of knowledge, skill, attitude, and values.

Chapter 3

LIFE SKILLS AND COMPETENCIES

3.1 Life Skills

Life skills education has a long history of supporting child development and health promotion. In 1986, the Ottawa Charter for Health Promotion recognized life skills in terms of making better health choices. The 1989 Convention on the Rights of the Child (CRC) linked life skills to education by stating that education should be directed towards the development of the child's fullest potential. The 1990 Jomtien Declaration on 'Education for All' took this vision further and included life skills among the essential learning tools for survival, capacity development, and quality of life. The Dakar World Education Conference in 2000 took the position that all young people and adults have the human right to benefit from 'an education that includes learning to know, to do, to live together and to be', and underlined the need of life skills education.

Life skills education is now recognized as a methodology to address diverse issues of child and youth development and thematic responses in UNGASS (United Nations General Assembly Special Session) on HIV/AIDS (2001), UNGASS on Children (2002), World Youth Report (2003), World Program of Human Rights Education (2004), UN Decade on Education for Sustainable Development (2005), UN Secretary General's Study on Violence Against Children (2006), 51st Commission on the Status of Women (2007), the World Development Report (2007), UNESCO Approach paper on Education (2015), etc. In India, various policies on education, children, adolescent, and youth categorically mention the importance and need for life skills development like population policy (1976), women empowerment policy (1990), health policy (1983), skill development policy (2009), youth policy (2014), National Education Policy (2020), etc.

The International Bureau of Education (IBE) derives its understanding on/of education from the Delors' Commission Report (1996) i.e. Four Pillars of Learning - learning to know, learning to do, learning to be, and learning to live together- and defines life skills as 'personnel management and social skills which are necessary for adequate functioning of individuals on an independent basis' (Delors, 1996, P. 22).

According to WHO, (1997 p.1) "It is a person's ability to maintain a state of mental well-being and to demonstrate this in adaptive and positive behaviour while interacting with others, in his/her culture and environment". Life skills are defined as the "ability that can be imbibed and improved through practise to translate the knowledge attitude and values into positive behaviour, to deal efficiently with the needs and challenges of everyday life" (WHO 1997a, p.1). WHO (1997) further adds that life skills are the abilities for adaptive and positive behaviour that enable individuals to deal effectively with the demands and challenges of everyday life. Life skills are defined in the Targeting Life Skills (TLS) Model (Hendricks, 1996) as "Skills that help an individual to be successful in living a productive and satisfying life."

Life skills are regarded as a cross-cutting, interconnected, and overlapping application of knowledge, values, attitudes, and skills which are integral to quality education and are universally applicable and contextual. The development of life skills is a process to be applied to various learning areas covering four dimensions: the cognitive, the individual, the social, and the instrumental (UNICEF-MENA, 2017). Life skills are defined by UNICEF as cognitive and non-cognitive, higher-order, transversal and transferrable skills for learning, for employability, for personal empowerment, and for active citizenship.

A skill is a learned ability to do something well. So, life skills are the abilities that individuals can develop to live a fruitful life. Life skills are psychosocial abilities that enable individuals to translate knowledge, attitudes, and values regarding their concerns into well-informed and healthy behaviour. Life skills are accepted as valuable and worthwhile, can effectively influence the development of academic success, peer relationships, family relationships, employment, extracurricular leisure activities, and positive attitude towards life (Kaur and Singh, 2015).

Life skills play a great role in enabling adolescents in enabling fruitful and healthy citizens of tomorrow, helping them to handle challenges and face the challenges of day-to-day life in a healthier, programmatic, and constructive way. Empowered with such skills, young people are able to take decisions based on a logical process of "what to do, why to do, how to do and when to do".

A positive attitude is essential to cope with the rapid changes which happen in the life of a young adolescent in the areas of body, mind, and soul. Different values need to be experienced at different levels and internalized through development of appropriate expression. Social skills are needed to use values throughout the day. Young people need to think about them, reflect on them and carry them into their personal and social lives. They need to be able to see the effect of their behaviour and choices and develop into socially conscious citizens. One can develop Knowledge, Attitudes, Value Enhanced Life Skills (KAVELS), accurately, objectively, and scientifically.

3.2   Core Life Skills

Core life skills are essential skills that young people need to be fully prepared to work in a global economy. It is sometimes referred to as deep learning. These are the 21ˢᵗ century skills that young people require for new ways of working, new ways of thinking and new ways of living in a global world. These skills are needed in many work environments. Life skills empower young people to take positive action, to protect themselves and promote healthy and positive social relationships.

Life skills are abilities that make differences in everyday living and help a person to perceive and respond effectively to significant events. These skills give a person self-direction and protection to lead a satisfactory life and contribute to society. They enable a person to function effectively in a changing world, to explore alternative ways, pros and cons, and make rational decisions in solving each problem or issue, as it arises. They help to establish interpersonal relationships with others and educate others to fight poverty and vulnerability, communicate effectively, to say no and to be assertive and decisive in solving problems.

There are numerous skills that can be categorized as life skills and the nature and definition of life skills differs across cultures and settings. But there is a core set of skills that are at the centre of skills-based initiatives for the promotion of health and well-being of children and adolescents and help in competence development in youngsters. After long deliberations with various UN agencies, WHO has come out with ten core life skills namely: self-awareness, empathy, creative thinking, critical thinking, decision-making, problem-solving, effective communication, interpersonal relationships, coping with stress and coping with emotions.

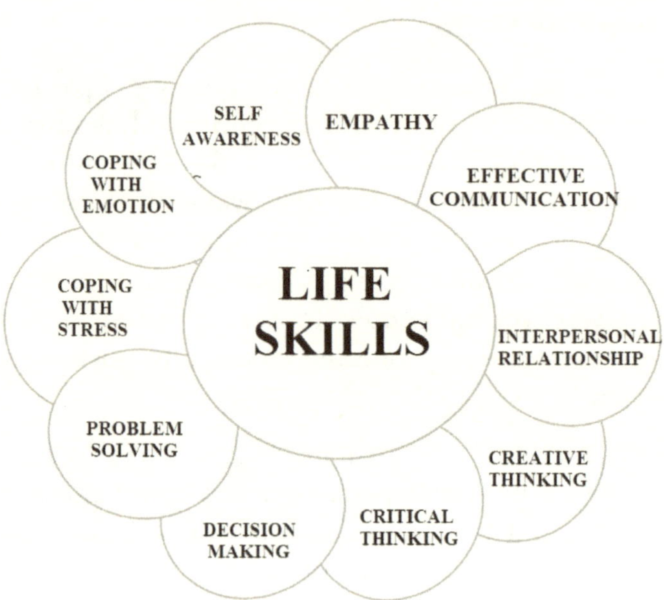

Figure 3.1: *Graphic representation of core life skills (Source: Self)*

1. **Self-awareness**: self-awareness means the recognition of 'self' and it is the awareness about oneself (self-consciousness). It makes the students understand their strengths, weaknesses, opportunities, threats, insecurities, likes, and dislikes. It helps the students to comprehend his/her self-worth, self-value and develop the confidence to face the challenges of life boldly. Developing self-awareness can help students to recognize their stress or the feeling of being under pressure. It enables one to identify one's weaknesses or negative personality traits and consequently helps the person to work on him/herself and improve oneself.

2. **Empathy**: It is the ability to understand and accept one's feelings, emotions, problems, and difficulties. Empathy is our mental ability to accept others without any prejudices and biases and to imagine what life is like for another person, even in a situation that we may not be familiar with. It enables a person to understand the feelings of others in distress and helps in reaching out and in providing emotional support to them. Empathy encourages nurturing behaviour for those who need care and assistance. Empathy can help a student

to know and accept others. They may be very different and from diverse cultures and origins. It encourages them to be genuinely interested in people who are in need of care and assistance and tolerance.

3. **Effective Communication:** Effective communication is described as the ability to express oneself, both verbally and non-verbally, in ways that are appropriate to our culture and situations. It is the ability to communicate clearly and precisely. It enables an adolescent to clearly express his/her opinion, needs, desire, and fears by using both verbal communication and non-verbal expressions. A person with good communication skills learns to listen actively to others and is aware of the importance of understanding what others are saying.

4. **Interpersonal Relationships:** Interpersonal skills help to initiate and maintain a positive relationship with other individuals. Relating with others is an important life skill and one of the most important forms of human intelligence and is called, people skills. This provides warmth, care, support, and collaboration that gives life. Interpersonal relationships teach the students to know the importance of maintaining and sustaining a positive relationship with other people. It also enables students to end relationships constructively. It enables people to work and live in diverse cultures.

5. **Creative Thinking:** Creative thinking is the ability to generate innovative ideas and translates them from abstract thought into/to reality. It is a novel way of seeing and doing things. It enables the students to be innovative and think out of the box. It consists of ideas, shifting perspective easily, conceiving something new and building on other ideas. Creative thinking is typically used to refer to the act of generating new ideas, approaches or actions. It helps an adolescent to respond in a flexible manner to various challenges of life and adapt to change quickly. It enables him /her to explore the possibilities and available alternatives, to assess their consequences and to create original ideas to guide them, and to look for new perspectives.

6. **Critical Thinking:** Critical thinking is self-directed and self-disciplined thinking, based on logical reasoning and objectivity. It is the ability to explore the various sources of information and how to apply them to particular problems, and to analyze them rationally, both sides without judging. Critical thinking improves the quality of thinking by taking charge of the structures inherent in thinking and imposing intellectual standards upon them. Critical thinking enables a person to analyze information and experiences logically and objectively. It also helps to recognize and assess the factors that influence attitudes and behaviour, such as values, peer pressure, and media. This skill helps in both problem-solving and decision-making

7. **Decision Making**: It is the ability to deal constructively with important issues in our lives and take appropriate decisions and actions. It helps to choose the best amongst the various alternatives or opinions in many life situations. It is the skill to analyze the pros and cons of alternatives and to accept responsibility for the consequences of the decision with confidence. It guides students to take decisions on the basis of facts and shoulder responsibility to face the consequences.

8. **Problem Solving:** Problem solving is the ability to solve a problem constructively and to understand that problems are inevitable. This skill assists in resolving a conflict and reaching a solution. It develops the ability to get out of difficult situations and achieve the goal without using anger, coercion, defiance and aggressive behavior. Problem solving is a process that provides an opportunity for a positive act. It enables a student to solve the problem by adopting creative and critical thinking.

9. **Coping with Emotions:** Coping with emotions assists a person to know his own feelings and those of others and respond appropriately to those emotions. The skill makes a person understand that strong feelings are normal and that feelings are neutral. Acceptance of feelings is the first step to control them; this enables a person to learn healthy, positive,

and safe ways to express their feelings and also increases the ability to identify his or her emotions. It helps students to know the effect of emotions on behaviour and learn to react to emotions appropriately. Students learn the techniques to control excessive emotions like anger and sorrow. They understand the adverse effect of negative emotions if one does not respond appropriately.

10. **Coping with Stress**: Coping with stress makes a person identify the source of stress and stressful situations in life. It also enables a person to understand the effects of stress and how to relax before the situation worsens. It helps in gaining strength to cope with positive or negative stressful situations. It enables a person to deal with accompanying emotions. In looking for the most beneficial solution, this skill enables the students to recognize the sources of stress, effects of stress, techniques to control stress and overcome it.

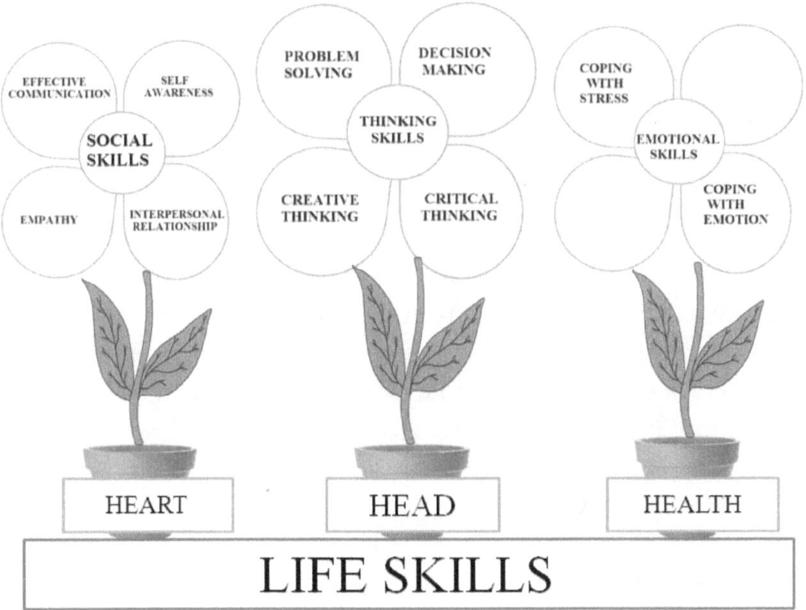

Figure 3.2: Classification of life skills (Source: Self)

3.3   Classification of Life Skills

Social Skills

Self-awareness, empathy, interpersonal relationships, and communication skills are classified as social skills. Adolescents need social skills for building positive and healthy relationships with others including a peer of the opposite sex. They need to understand the importance of mutual respect and socially defined boundaries in every relationship. Social skills are the skills that we use to interact and communicate with others, every day. They include verbal and non-verbal communication, such as speech, gestures, facial expressions, and body language. Developing social skills is about being aware of how we communicate with others. Social skills facilitate strengthening relationships by helping adolescents to understand themselves, appreciate the importance of friends and family, and helping them to improve their communication skills. The social skills of children are effectively seen when they participate in games, communicate and help each other (Oden and Asher, 1997).

Social skills are crucial in making and sustaining friendships and are vital in enabling an individual to have and maintain positive interactions with others. It is imperative that individuals have 'empathy' as this allows them to respond in an understanding and caring way to how others are feeling (Masters and Furman, 1981). Social interactions do not always run smoothly and an individual needs to be able to implement appropriate strategies, such as conflict resolutions when difficulties in interactions arise. Human beings are sociable and develop many ways to communicate their messages, thoughts, and feeling with others (La Greca, & Santogrossi, 1980).

Thinking Skills

Thinking skills are decision-making and problem-solving which include understanding the consequences of the actions, and determining alternative solutions to problems. Evaluating one's perceptions of social norms and beliefs; self-evaluation and clarification of values fall under critical thinking. Creative thinking is also one of the most important skills of thinking skills. These skills help in understanding the physical, physiological, mental, and emotional changes during puberty, thereby helping adolescents to cope with these changes and help them plan their life.

Thinking skills promote effective questioning and extend oral responses. Creative thinking has implications on the intellectually disciplined process of actively and skillfully conceptualizing, applying, analyzing, synthesizing, and evaluating information gathered from, or generated by, observation, experience, reflection, reasoning, or communication, as a guide to belief and action. Creative thinking results in openness, flexibility, autonomy, playfulness, humour, willingness to take risks, and perseverance. Creative and critical thinking is effective in improving mental, physical, behavioral health and competence among adolescents. (Karger et al., 2013)

Coping Skills

Coping skills are characteristics or behavioural patterns that enhance a person's adaptation. It is a strategy used to manage intense emotional experiences. They do not solve the problem or help to remove the problem; instead, they help to tolerate or manage the problem. They include managing stress, regulating emotions, and skills for increasing internal locus of control (self-management and self-monitoring).

Negotiation Skills

Negotiation skills help in problem-solving, decision-making, and maintaining positive relationships. It also helps adolescents adopt hygienic practises, improve their nutritional status and choose to eat wisely. These skills include self-awareness, effective verbal communication, listening, interpersonal relationships, reducing misunderstanding, rapport building, problem-solving and decision making, being assertive, and dealing with difficult situations.

3.4 Philosophical and Theoretical Underpinnings of Life Skills

The two landmark UNESCO publications, 'Learning to Be' known as 'Faure Report' (1972), and Learning: The Treasure Within' or 'Delors Report' (1996) recognize that lifelong learning is integral to a meaningful human life. They have been influential in promoting an integrated and humanistic vision of lifelong learning.

Faure report stressed firmly, establishing the concept of lifelong education at a time when traditional education systems were being changed (Faure et al. 1972). In this interpretation, life skills emphasize both whole-person development and a life-long learning perspective, i.e., learning throughout life. The title, learning to be, focuses on the human condition and on the role of education in the development of every individual's potential. This report recommends that one no longer tirelessly acquires knowledge once and for all, but learns how to build up a continually evolving body of knowledge all through life - 'learning to be'. Lifelong education is the master concept for educational policies. It is not an educational system but the principle in which the overall organization of a system is found.

Life skills are captured in the simplest and deepest way in the four pillars of learning of the Delors report (Delors et al. 1996), with outcomes of education relating to four crucial areas affecting a self-fulfilling life and contribution to societal development. They are (1) learning to know, which means to master the instruments of knowledge, (2) learning to do, which is to apply knowledge into practice, (3) learning to live together and living with others means to prevent and resolve conflicts and promote peace and respect for other people, their cultures and spiritual values and (4) learning to be, is to ensure all-round development of each individual (Buchert, 2014). Since then, two additional pillars have been suggested at the first World Forum on Lifelong Learning held in Paris in 2008: learning for change and transformation; and learning to become. Because of the rapid changes which are taking place in countries, regions, and the world in general and in the life of individuals throughout their lifetime, it constitutes a continuous process of forming whole beings - their knowledge, aptitudes, critical faculty, and ability to act.

Child and Adolescent Development Theory

The concept of child and adolescent development was developed by Piaget (1972) and further developed by Vygotsky (1978). These two researchers have made a foundation in developing and understanding the behavioural matrix as well as other developmental aspects extensively. Learning to realistically evaluate oneself and one's abilities is another important process during childhood (Newman and Newman, 1999). Piaget believed that an adolescent person is able to conceptualize many variables and able to create a system of laws or rules for problem-solving (Piaget, 1972). Social interactions become increasingly complicated as children move into adolescence. More time is spent with peers and interactions with the opposite sex increases. During these critical years, children either learn to be competent or productive or feel inferior, which can lead to long-lasting social, intellectual emotional consequences (Hansen et al., 1998; Csikszentmihalyi and Schneider, 2000). Moral development is an important dimension of human development.

Social Learning Theory

This theory, which is also known as the Cognitive-Social Learning Model, is largely based upon the works of Albert Bandura (Bandura, 1977). Children learn to behave through observation and social interaction rather than just through verbal instructions. Their behaviour is reinforced, or modified, by the consequences of their actions and the responses of others to their behaviour. According to social learning theory, skill teaching needs to replicate the natural processes by which children learn behaviour, modelling, observation and social interaction. It further reinstates that reinforcement is important in learning and shaping behaviour.

Social Influence Theory

Social influence approaches are based upon the work of Bandura as well as the psychological inoculation theory developed by researchers, including McGuire (1964, 1968). Social influence approaches recognize that children and adolescents will come under pressure to engage in risk behaviour, such as tobacco use. By adopting the approach of social learning theory, peer and social pressure to engage in unhealthy behaviour, can be controlled by addressing them before the child or adolescent is exposed to the pressures. This points towards early prevention rather than later intervention. Teaching children that resistance is more effective in reducing behavioural problem years than just providing information or provoking fear of the results of behaviour (WHO, 2003).

Cognitive Problem Solving

The competence-building model proposed by Shure and Spivack (1980) theorizes the teaching Interpersonal Cognitive Problem Solving (ICPS) skills of children. Young age can reduce and prevent negative, inhibited and impulsive behaviour. The relationship between these problem-solving skills and social adjustment was not only found in the pre-school and kindergarten children, but also in adolescents and adults. An intervention based on his research, the ICPS intervention (also called "I can Problem Solve"), develops interpersonal cognitive problem -solving skills starting in preschool, with the ultimate goal of preventing later and more serious problems by addressing the behavioural predictors in the early stages of life.

Problem Behaviour Theory

Developed by Richard Jessor, it recognizes that adolescent behaviour (including risk behaviour) cannot be reduced to a single source. It is the product of complex interactions between people and their environment. The personality system includes 'values, expectations, beliefs, attitudes and orientations toward self and society'. According to this theory, activities are influenced by an individual's values, beliefs and attitudes and by the perceptions of friends and family about these types of behaviour. Therefore, skills in critical thinking (including the ability to evaluate oneself and the values of the social environment), effective communication, and negotiation are important aspects of skill-based education and life skills. Building these types of interactions into activities with opportunities to practise the skills is an important part of the learning process (WHO, 2003).

Multiple Intelligence Theory

The theory of multiple intelligences has important implications for the education system. Gardner (1993) suggested that all human beings are born with eight intelligences that take into account the wide variety of human thinking capacities. These include linguistic, logical/mathematical, musical, spatial bodily/kinesthetic, naturalist, interpersonal and intrapersonal intelligence. Classroom instruction focuses on linguistic and logical/mathematical abilities but in order to develop the eight multiple intelligences, children need to be exposed to effective teaching/learning processes and a broader range of indoor and outdoor activities which will bring out the talents that are hidden in them. Different varieties of activities will stimulate the children to be themselves and express themselves beyond academics. The involvement of children in active learning methods stimulates the use of musical, spatial, naturalist and other intelligences (Mangrulkar et al., 2001). Multiple intelligence is developed in a different degree in each individual depending on the use of their intelligence at different levels.

Emotional Intelligence

According to Goleman (1997), there are five main elements of emotional intelligence i.e., self-awareness, self-realization, motivation, empathy, and social skills. Emotional intelligence is the ability to understand and manage emotions in an effective manner. Anyone with higher levels of emotional intelligence is able to manage their emotions and relate to others around them as well as use their emotions to facilitate their thinking and understand the emotions of others. This can help to improve self-motivation, effective communication skills, and confident learners.

The community service learning framework is designed, based on the theory of emotional intelligence, to bring out life skills especially coping with emotions and coping with stress. When children come in touch with the community, they develop social skills as they interact with the community and as they get in deeper into the needs of the community. The children are led into deeper reflection on the unjust structures that prevails in the community; they become aware of themselves and society which enhances the development of their emotional skills. Emotional intelligence is emphasized in community service learning because students are constantly working with their peers and with community members.

The meaningful learning theory was founded by David Ansubel. Meaningful learning is that learned information is completely understood and can now be used to make connections with other previously known knowledge, aiding in further understanding. This type of learning is relational and links new information to existing knowledge. It is active, constructive, and durable. Teachers need to demonstrate to the students what students do not know. It implies understanding. It helps them to achieve deep learning instead of rote learning. When the facts are meaningful, it makes sense to the students and they are able to retain the information a lot better. The most crucial element in meaningful learning is how the new information is integrated into the old knowledge structure. Community service learning is integrated into the school curriculum to deliver meaningful learning among students as they practise abstract knowledge, and use meaningfully what they have already learned in their text.

3.5   Approaches in Life Skills Education

An approach means a general philosophy and strategy and is a careful plan or method for achieving a particular goal. The life skills approach refers to a good interactive education methodology. It uses a wide variety of participatory and interactive techniques. It is a comprehensive multi-strategy approach. The goal of this approach is to promote healthy, sociable behaviour and to prevent or reduce risk behaviours as well as make a positive impact on knowledge and attitude. Life skills education should not be looked into as a subject but viewed as a process fitting within the framework of four pillars of education namely learning to know, learning to do, to live together, and learning to be.

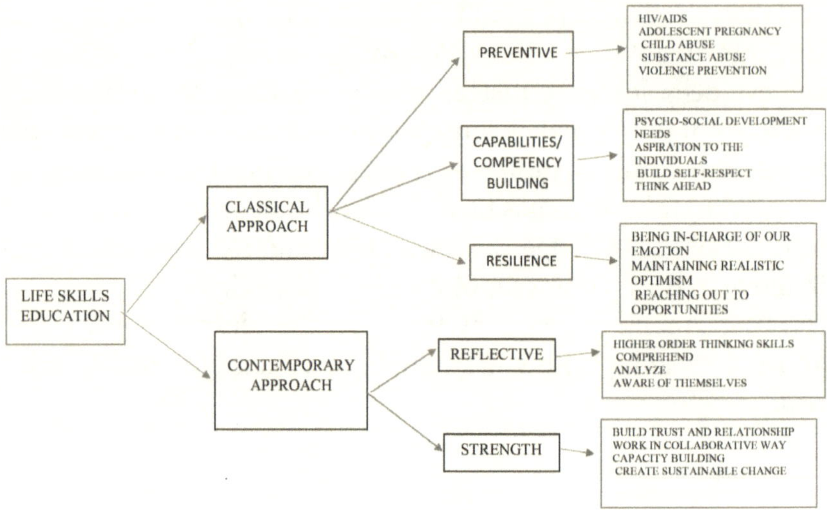

Figure 3.3: *Diagram showing approaches in life skills education (Source: self)*

- These approaches can be classified under two broad categories namely the classified approach and the contemporary approach.

- The classified approach encompasses the preventive approach, the competency approach, and the resiliency approach whereas the contemporary approach encompasses the reflective thinking approach and the strength-based approach.

- Classical approaches are mostly taught by a developed training module, guest lectures, brainstorming methods, working in small groups, and role play to practise the skills (Gulhane, 2014).

- Reflective thinking approach and strength-based approaches can lead to the holistic development of a person (Ranjan, & Nair, 2015).

- Community service learning could be considered as reflective thinking and a strength-based approach as children who are actively engaged in civic responsibility activities improve their life skills and competencies.

3.6 Life skills Education and its Importance

Life skills education promotes mental well-being in young people and empowers adolescents to take more responsibility for their actions. The pedagogy of life skills education is experiential learning. It influences psychological health, attitudes, and values leading to positive behaviour and it helps to prevent risk behaviour (Nori, 1998). Life skills education is designed to help one to process and structure one's experiences and facilitate the practise and reinforcement of skills

- "Life skills education is designed to facilitate the practise and reinforcement of psychological skills in a culturally and developmentally appropriate way. It contributes to the promotion of personal and social development, the prevention of health and social problem, and the protection of human rights" (WHO 1999).

- Life skills enable people to deal with challenging situations positively and successfully. It helps to assess oneself and become aware of one's strengths and weaknesses. A continuous process of realization challenges to change one's attitude towards family members and neighbors. It develops the social, individual, and reflective skills of the people.

- Life skills enhance abilities that help to facilitate communication, negotiation, to think critically, solving problems, and make independent decisions (Usha Rao, 2016).

- Life skills education addresses the combination of psychological and social (i.e. psychosocial) factors that contribute to healthy behaviour. The promotion of personal and social skills is an important aspect of health promotion interventions that aim to empower the individual to promote his/her own health as well as the health of others and of the community (Prajapati, Sharma and Sharma. 2017).

- Life skills education introduces learner-centered and interactive teaching methods which can have a positive impact on the relationships between teachers and pupils, young people's enjoyment of learning, teacher job satisfaction, rates of dropout, and absenteeism from school (Rani and Menka 2019).

- Life skills have an impact on the teaching of academic subjects. There are indications that life skills education can have a positive impact on academic performance. Once the students feel that they are involved in issues of relevance to their own lives, they participate more and learn more.

- Life skills education can promote more pro-social behaviour and so results in less delinquency among adolescents. It helps to clarify the needs of young people growing up in modern societies.

- Life skills education is of particular value to young people growing up in multicultural societies and the skills promoted, appear to be amongst the ones most highly valued by the future employers of young people. Early prevention can be expected to reap maximum rewards in regard to a healthy society since the health and social problems prevalent today have at their root a component of human behaviour.

- The child in the present education system, which works like a factory, is considered a product because there is no personal touch. Therefore, the personal growth and development of the child are overlooked (Kurian, 2015). Since information is available at the click of a button, at this juncture it is very important to equip young people with the right information which will help them to make informed decisions (Parida, 2015).

- Adolescents need help and guidance in decision-making, problem-solving, critical thinking, developing interpersonal relationships, self-awareness, coping with stress, and coping with emotions. In the fast-growing incidents of conflicts and crisis, smoking, drinking, tobacco use, and other substance abuse, suicides, crimes, and risk behaviour among adults are matters of great concern (Bharath and Kumar, 2008). Life skills are very important in this regard as they enable individuals to translate knowledge and attitudes into actual abilities.

- The central goal of life skills education is to empower adolescents and envision them to attain a meaningful and healthy life (Pujar and Patil, 2016). Life skills education provides an integrated and holistic approach to adolescent development and it is based on a framework where 'core life skills' include thinking skills, social skills, and emotional skills (Parvathy and Pillai, 2015).

- Life skills education is designed to facilitate the practise and reinforcement of psychological skills in a culturally and developmentally appropriate way. It contributes to the promotion of personal and social development, the prevention of health and social problems, and the protection of human rights (WHO 1999).

- Recent researches show that the life skills competencies of the young, are not adequate to address the challenges of the 21st century (Deffenbacher, Lynch, Crede and Kuncel, 2008; Rao, 2011). To prepare the pupils to face the challenges of daily life, life skills education has to be introduced as a special subject in school due to that they will respond effectively to the needs of the contemporary world (Mahmoudi & Moshayedi, 2012).

- Life skills education promotes mental well-being in young people and empowers adolescents to take more responsibility for their actions (Nasheeda, 2019). The Central Board of Secondary Education (CBSE), an autonomous body under the Ministry of Education, Government of India, New Delhi, reinforces life skills, sports, and games, co-curricular activities as a part of mainstream education, and emphasis is laid on the need to include life skills education for co-scholastic assessment of the student. The schools are now mandated to provide and also assess students on parameters of life skills (Parmar and Katoch, 2015) but in many schools, the life skills lessons are not handled properly and there are no trained teachers to impart life skills (Daisy and Nair, 2018).

3.7   The Relevance of 21ˢᵗ Century Life Skills

There are many of us who have high qualifications but not necessarily all of us are skilled enough. In this scenario, we need to emphasize on teaching 21ˢᵗ century skills besides the academic syllabus which will enable the students to cope with the uncertainty of life and all unprecedented situations like the pandemic. 21ˢᵗ century skills can be applied in all academic subject areas, and in all educational, career, and civic settings throughout a student's life. If we train our students in life skills, it will enable them to absorb the 21ˢᵗ century skills such as critical thinking, problem-solving, reasoning, analysis, interpretation, synthesizing information, research skills and practises, interrogative questioning, creativity, artistry, curiosity, imagination, innovation, personal expression, perseverance, self-direction, planning, self-discipline, adaptability, initiative, oral and written communication, public speaking and presenting, listening, leadership, teamwork, collaboration, cooperation, facility in using virtual workspaces, information and communication technology (ICT) literacy, media and internet literacy, data interpretation and analysis, computer programming, civic, ethical, and social-justice literacy, economic and financial literacy, entrepreneurship. Global awareness, multicultural literacy, humanitarianism, scientific literacy and reasoning, the scientific method, environmental and conservation literacy, ecosystems understanding, health, and wellness literacy including nutrition, diet, exercise, and public health and safety. These skills will keep changing as the world keeps evolving. If structured community service learning is conducted with the teachers or community service learning coordinator's facilitation, we will be able to see children imbibing these skills.

Chapter 4

STRATEGY AND PROCESS

4.1 Development of a Community Service Learning Module

In this section, we will discuss the development of a community project as part of the service learning mission.

- A few rounds of discussions were held with the students of 9th standard in the selected school on the importance of community service learning and how it would change our lives and the community. Various social issues, community development programmes, civic engagement, and their duty as a citizen, were topics that were discussed.

- After the classroom discussion, they were taken out to visit the locality that was close to the school so that they could interact with the members of the community. This interaction helped them to understand the needs and concerns of the people. This experience enabled them to realize the problems of the community and how the people are coping with it in their daily life.

- The students brainstormed their experiences in the community and the needs and problems of the community. They asked many questions themselves and later arrived at a decision to do something. So, they voiced a few activities as a solution to the issues.

- The student-community interaction has helped me to understand the enthusiasm of the students in community work and their areas of interest as well as the needs of the community. In the meantime, the researcher familiarized herself with the 9th standard syllabus. The task was to link the activity to be taken up in the community with that of the syllabus that the students are learning. Thus, the researcher had developed the community service learning module considering the students' area of interest, the community's needs, and the relevant syllabus of the students in consultation with the supervising teacher.

- The activities were planned under five areas of concern such as health and mental well-being, education, hygiene and sanitation, environment, and skill development. It was designed to cover four hours and two hours of activity. Fifteen activities (three activities under each area of concern) of 2 hours including reflection, each activity is repeated twice which totals up to 60 hours and 5 activities (one activity under each area of concern) of 4 hours including reflection, also repeated twice which is a total of 40 hours. Overall, there are twenty activities which require 20 hours for preparation (one hour of preparation for each activity). So, 120 hours (60 hours of 2 hours activity + 40 hours of 4 hours activities + 20 hours for preparation for 20 activities = 120 hours) of community service learning activities were prepared. It is important to conduct long hours of community service learning during school hours and repeat each activity more than once so that the impact will be strengthened. Each activity included preparation and reflection.

- The module contained the objective of conducting a particular activity, with the theoretical knowledge the students need to know, the process that would be followed to carry out this activity, the resources required for the successful execution of the activity, and the learning outcome of the students. Great care was taken that children were not bored. This was to ensure joyful learning without physical exhaustion.

- The draft community service learning module was sent to a few of the experts in the subject of psychology, social work, and work education and a few school teachers who teach science and social studies to 9th standard students for their feedback. It was also shown to the principals of the schools and their permission was obtained to carry out the activity. The community service learning module was checked with a few community members about the feasibility of carrying out certain activities.

- Feedback from different experts was taken into consideration and it was found to be very valuable as it added meaning to the module. The community service learning module was pilot-studied in one of the schools among the 9th standard students and found feasible and actionable. The children understood the concept and interacted well with the community members, in addition to enjoying the activity. In this way, the community service learning module was standardized. The areas of intervention are health and mental wellbeing, education, hygiene and sanitation, environment, and skill development. The framework of the community service module is given in Annexure 1.

4.2 Community Service Learning Framework

The community service learning framework consists of six features such as orientation, investigation/identification, planning and preparation, action, reflection, and evaluation. A well-structured community service learning activities ensure its success.

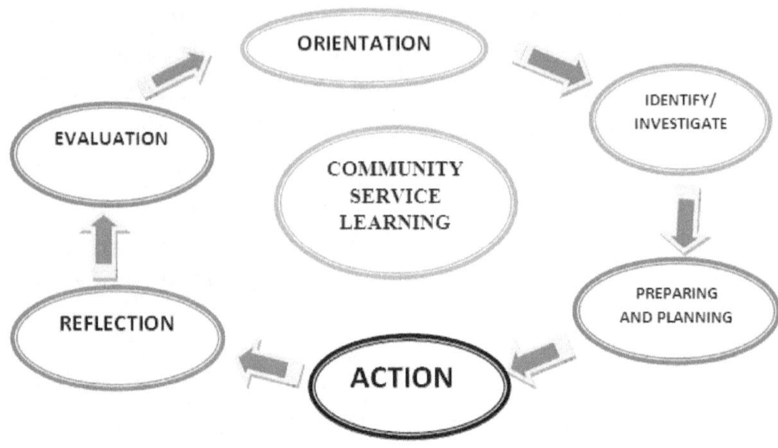

Figure 4.1: *Framework of community service learning (Source: Self)*

The basic framework of community service learning includes:

Orientation

The school management needs to understand the meaning and impact of community service learning and hence orientation training is organized. The school administration organizes an orientation with training for the staff on how to design the service activities and facilitate the children to execute community service learning. A session is also arranged for the parents of the students who are participants in the community service learning and get the consent form (Annexure-II) as their children will be involved in outdoor activities. The teacher gets written permission from the school management and contacts the members of the community and informs them about students' involvement in community development-related issues. The teacher arranges an orientation programme to explain to the students the significance of community service learning and its importance.

Identify/Investigation

After the introduction to the community service learning programme and its concept, the teacher visits the school surroundings and gets familiarized with the locality. They identify a few areas of concern and the school administration makes an agreement that the children will work with the community to solve a few issues of the community. The students are taken to the community and encouraged to interact with people and to observe the surroundings and living conditions of the community; especially they are guided to find out the needs and problems of the community. With the help of classroom discussions, the teacher helps the students to identify the issues related to the community and society at large and particularly the community in the school vicinity. The issues that the people face in the community are noted and the root causes of the problems are analyzed.

> Students visited the neighbouring school community and observed papers and plastics littered around. The students realized that it could be cleaned and the waste could be separated by using a solid waste management system and compost pit.

Planning and Preparation

The community service learning project is designed after identifying the needs of the community. To make the community service learning experience more enriching and learning, the teacher reads the syllabus of the class and becomes familiar with all the subjects and their interdisciplinary features. The teacher and the students relate the community issues with the academic knowledge that they study in the classroom. The following questions are asked before planning the process and the execution of the activity. These questions would lead to in-depth Action Research through which students would collectively, be able to suggest measures for remediation of the existing problem. What are the problems? What can be done to bring about positive changes in the community? How to carry out the activity? Who will do what work? What is the time duration? Students are instructed well on the theoretical connection with the subject and the activities that will help them to solve the problems of the community. They are divided into groups and given sufficient time to prepare for the activity before they go to the community to execute the action. The learning objectives are planned based on the activity and theoretical knowledge. The activities are designed to be fun learning and not boring. The time duration is well taken care of so that the students are not physically stressed.

- Students read more about the theoretical concept of sanitation, waste management, and compost pit.

- Students were divided into small groups and discussed how to plan and prepare, how to reach out to the community.

- They decided to organize a swachchada march; for which placards were prepared with catchy slogans.

- They decided to write a letter to the local municipality to request dustbins to segregate the waste.

- They learn how to prepare compost pits and collect the materials required for it and communicate to the community, the materials they can get from them.

- The community members were informed about the swachchada march and ensured their participation. Trained the community members in solid waste management system and how to prepare compost pits.

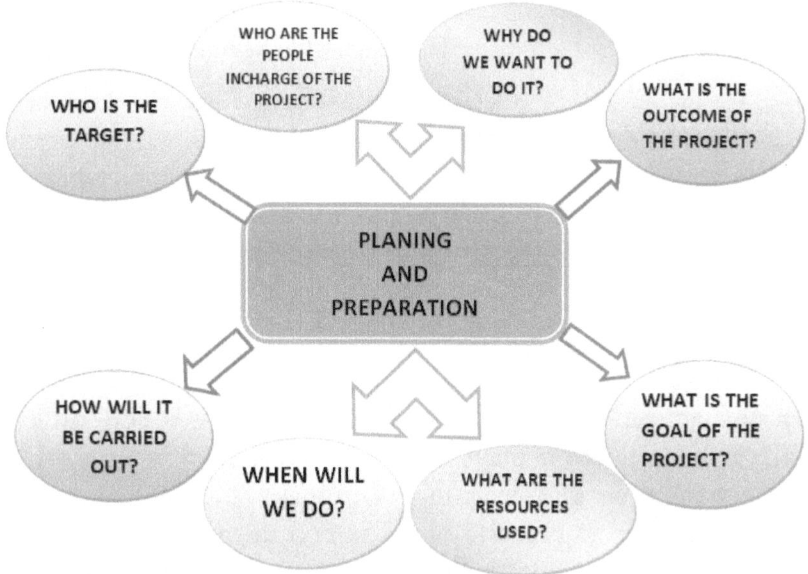

Figure 4.2: *Planning and preparation of community service learning (Source: Self)*

Action

Students went to the community and interacted with the members about the project and convinced the members that they needed their help and support to carry out the action that was planned. All the plans are executed with the community, where community members become partners with the children. The students work in groups. If there is a possibility, different NGOs, agencies and parents of the children are invited to be a part of it. Action is for the welfare of the community. The students apply what they have learned in the classroom. It is the role of the faculty to see that the students are challenged to be more creative and imaginative to exercise what they have learned. If the planned action is not done within the stipulated time and it is carried forward to another day, the faculty has to make sure that it is completed.

> - Students go for the Swachchada march with the community members.
>
> - Fix the dustbins in a few places where people live and show them what materials go to which dustbin such as paper, plastic, food waste, bottles, metal waste, etc.
>
> - Prepared a compost pit with the community members.

Reflection

On the action being performed, the students spend time in reflection. Reflection plays a critical role and acts as a bridge between service and learning (Dubinsky J, 2006). Activities are designed to enable students to ponder and evaluate their experience, consider its value and transform it into knowledge. The students grow in greater awareness, broadening his/her horizons of knowledge; understanding divergent viewpoints, and perspectives of the poor, marginalized and disadvantaged, and oppressed categories of society. Reflection is an essential part of community service learning and it fosters meaning in the student's ability to make meaning from experience which results in creative thinking. Reflection contributes to moral reasoning and generates new and improved action. Reflection supports the development of civic outcomes. Reflection is thinking intentionally about an experience, gaining understanding or insight, and results in taking new actions.

> - After finishing the activity, the students spent a few minutes in silence to introspect on how they conducted themselves during the whole process of community service learning; how it has affected their life personally.
>
> - They took the notes on their reflection and the learning experience during the community learning service.

Evaluation

Evaluation is about recording what has been implemented. The students need to spend time on reflection and evaluation of the entire process. Since students look for appreciation, it has to be celebrated. It is important to conduct an evaluation or assessment to see if any modifications or revisions are required. The faculty should foster relationships of mutual trust and respect which set a climate for discussion and growth. Useful evaluative processes include mentoring and reviews of students' journals, as well as students' self-evaluation in light of personal growth profiles. Internal or external feedback may serve to launch the learners to continuity and multiplication of service learning projects. Regular feedback from school management, teachers, parents, and members of the community will help to design high-quality community service learning projects. It leads the participants to think about the service performed and its impact on the community, considering what worked well and what could be changed to make the project better.

- Take a quick review of what happened from the beginning to the end of the activity.

- Celebrate with the children what has been achieved.

- Ask the students what could be done better if they do the same activity again?

- Note down the learning and appreciate and encourage the children.

4.3 The Effect of Community Service Learning

The school can play a key role in developing life skills by making life skills education a part of the school curriculum because there is a decrease in moral values, high insecurity, and negative thoughts in our upcoming generation (Ajith Kumar & Nair 2015). It is important for students to develop skills for the application of knowledge, teamwork, and civic engagement in addition to core curriculum knowledge to prepare for the demands of the 21st century workforce. Students would "learn by doing," applying knowledge to experience and developing skills or new ways of thinking (Lewis & Williams, 1994, p. 6).

The United Nations Children's Fund (UNICEF, 2005) reports that the content of life skills programming was not always relevant and appropriate and the methods used were not always effective, particularly with different types of learners. Many programmes have not given provisions to support learners in the use of their new life skills outside the classroom, to use with their families, or in their communities. To respond to the need of teaching life skills, many studies have been done in the field of life skills education adopting various strategies. The literature review shows that no study has been done in India on community service learning as an intervention to impart life skills.

Community service learning is experiential learning which focuses on learning to serve and serve to learn. It is an integrated programme within the school that can be introduced not as a separate activity; instead, students could apply their knowledge of what they have learned in the classroom for the benefit of the community.

Therefore, community service learning as a pedagogy of learning will help to develop the ten core life skills among children. The community service learning will enable the students to develop their reflective thinking and in turn, develop their life skills and competencies.

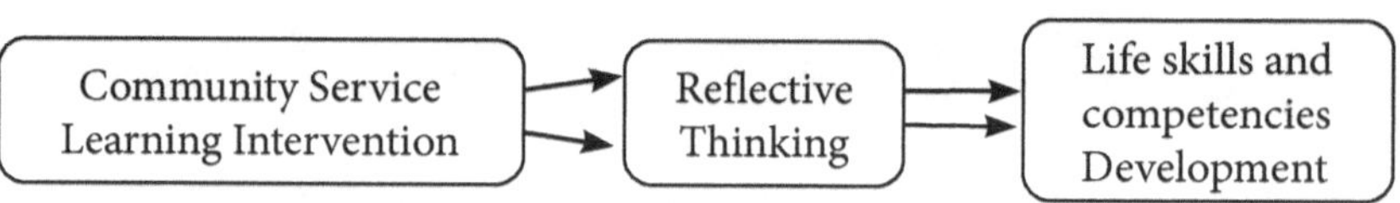

Figure 4.3: Effect of community service learning intervention (Source – Self)

4.4 Strategies in Community Service Learning to Factor in Life Skills Development

Community service learning is one of the many teaching strategies, that educators use to combine classroom instruction with community service. Students participate in the projects in their local community while applying the concepts that they learned in the classroom (Markus, Howard and King, 1993). It is an experimental practice that students require to apply to their theoretical knowledge. Community service learning is a collaborative teaching and learning strategy designed to promote academic enhancement, personal growth and civic engagement (He and Prater, 2014). The course design, which includes critical reflection, examines students' experiences critically and articulates specific learning outcomes, thus enhancing the quality of their learning and of their service (Ramsaroop and Ramdhani 2014). The difference is that the students do more than cleaning the surroundings of the community. It is an intentional learning experience. For example, if the students engage in community service learning they not only clear garbage from a stream, but they also provide a valuable service to the community. However, they learn to analyze, and discuss what they found, identify possible sources and share the results with the local population. They analyze the reason for its uncleanliness and how it can be reduced and reflect upon what they experienced. It was (Jensen, 2006) advocated that community service learning connects deeply to the school curriculum, offering students unique opportunities to acquire new skills as they learn responsibility, experience satisfaction, and provide benefit to the wider community (Lowery et al, 2006). It is a highly effective strategy for engaging students' interest in the curriculum and in their community. The service component and the learning component should complement each other and neither should be favoured at the expense of the other.

Community service learning is experiential learning that nurtures social and cognitive skills, improves problem-solving, team-building, leadership, communication and organizational skills (Demir, et al., 2014). Community service learning, as consistently reported by researchers, is a heightened sense of social responsibility. It develops a positive attitude towards adults and others, understanding and active exploration of careers, enhancing self-esteem and growth in moral development (Eyler, 2000). Community service learning experience encourages youth to feel more self-competent, to discover commonalities with a broad range of people, and a more encompassing and integrated understanding of social, moral and political issues (Yates and Younis, 1996). Kackar-Cam and Schmidt (2014, p.84) point out that, "Adolescents who are involved in out-of-time activities are more motivated and cognitively engaged in comparison to other contexts of their lives".

In community service learning, students have a chance to experience different types of activities that will help them to shape their career interests later in life (Coetzee, Bloemhoff, and Naude, 2011). Most adolescents will be able to come out of their nervousness or shyness and start to interact with people they do not know (Kiely, 2005). One of the most important benefits of community service is that it instills in students a strong feeling of self-worth. Community service learning gives students an experience in expressing their opinions in front of adults thereby increasing their confidence (Niemi, R.G et al., 2000). Camara (2012) explains in her research that students would learn more effectively and become better citizens if they are engaged in service to the community and have this service incorporated into their academic curriculum. Learning does not take place in the classroom alone, it takes place after school, on the weekends, on the playing fields, in the music room, and while students are performing community service. She has proved in her research the numerous benefits of community service learning such as growth in self-esteem, future engagement in political and civic interactions, creating a sense of citizenship, and above all improvement of the academic performance of the students. Community service learning is seen by the various boards of education as an integral part of education (Bettencourt, 2015; Tatebe, 2013).

Moreover, research has proved that community service as part of the school curriculum can eventually enhance meaningful value development (Hedin, 1989). In many Jesuit schools, community service learning is a common strategy for ensuring that graduating students who are open to growth, become intellectually competent, religious, loving, and committed to doing justice (O'Keefe, 2015). Students who are involved in social service programmes encounter themselves and others and find meaning in life (Su, Yuling and Chen, 2014). The students involved in community service learning activities gain a sense of social responsibility and a deeper understanding of the problem faced by the communities in which they serve (Koh et al., 2014). Students involved in community service learning reported that their fears and prejudices diminish with the experience of helping others (Herzberg, 1994).

4.5 Linkages of Community Service Learning with Life Skills Development

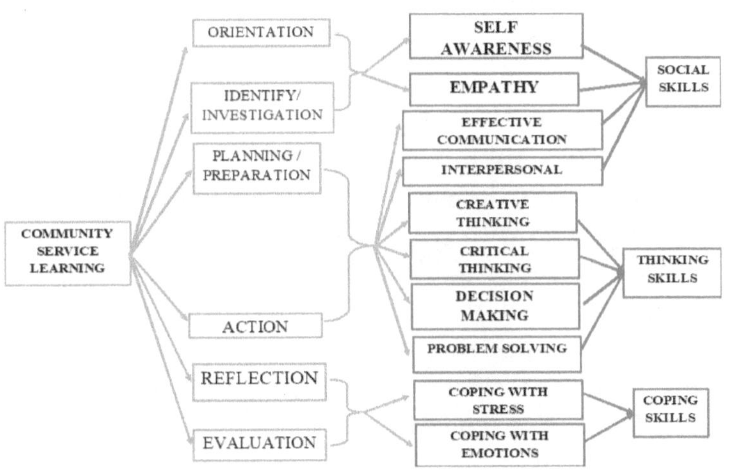

Figure 4.4: Linkage of community service learning with life skills development (Source – Self)

The impacts of community service learning are almost close to the ten core life skills. Therefore, we can take community service learning as a pedagogy to teach life skills in schools. Students who participate in community service learning reported that they were gaining career skills, communication skills and increases in career exploration knowledge, positive work orientation attitudes and had developed many other skills (Kendrick, 1996.; Billing, 2000). Community service learning helped students to become more knowledgeable and realistic about their careers. The teachers believed that participation in community service learning increased career awareness (Hamilton and Fenzel, 1988; Strage, 2000). The students improve in problem-solving skills and increase their interest in academics, engage more in their studies and get more motivated to learn (Parker-Gwin and Mabry, 1998.).

At the time of orientation, the teacher motivates and make the students realize the current situation and the reality of the world. The student become more aware of oneself and his/her surroundings. When the students visit the community to identify and investigate, they come to know the needs of the community. They empathize with the community and realize what they are capable of doing for them. As a result, they grow in self-awareness and empathy. During the time of planning and preparation, they tend to think creatively and critically to solve the problems and make a few decisions and plan how to execute them. During the period of action and implementation, they work in groups with their own peers and community and develop communication skills, interpersonal relationship skills, decision making, and the skills problem-solving. Reflection helps them personalize their own experience which gradually builds the emotional skills of coping with stress and time constraint. Evaluation enables the students to become aware of their own contribution to society, community, and to their peers. Through dialogue and interaction with teachers, peers, and community members, they develop self-awareness and enhance their communication and interpersonal skills. It increases critical thinking and problem analysis skills. They are involved in various activities which encourage them to develop competencies orientated toward collaborative and creative work, effective communication, decision-making and active participation in their community.

It illustrates the utility of community service learning as a framework for integration across all subjects. It could be considered as pedagogy to impart life skills (Parker-Gwin and Mabry 1996). It could be used as a guide to involving children in outdoor activities (Fisher, 2015). It will offer real-world experiences and the community, as the laboratory and all the activities could be connected to the existing syllabus.

Participation in community service learning is an educative activity by itself that helps in self-interrogation and enables the students to think more seriously about their lives (Rhoads, 1998). Community service learning may be seen as an "encounter with strangers" and it prepares students to communicate in a culturally diverse world (Radest, 1993). Community service learning may be mandated as part of the core curriculum so that all students have the opportunity to realize the relationship between community, civic involvement, and self-interest (Niemi et.al, 2000). The benefits of community-based learning activities are manifold (Koh et.al, 2014).

A network of life skills trainers provides life skills training to enhance skilled human capital (Ranjan and Nair, 2015). Not being aware of different approaches, many are resorting to classical approaches in life skills education. Several methods and strategies can be adopted for life skills education and training. Now-a-days, a strength-based approach is being used on a large scale for life skills education. Newer methods like drama, theater, sports, games, arts, etc. are used as a medium for life skills education (Vranda and Rao, 2011). Community service learning is one unexplored area to develop life skills and a strength-based approach to life skills as the foundation for life skills training. Community service learning is a tool for imparting life skills. Therefore, the researcher adopted it as a pedagogy of learning the ten-core life skills among children.

4.6 Challenges Faced while Implementing Community Service Learning

Optimal learning happens when we are challenged and stretched beyond what we already know and are comfortable with. Although there are many positive outcomes when students are involved in community service, there are also many obstacles and problems faced while carrying out these activities. The process of implementing it as part of the school curriculum is difficult as it involves many challenges:

- Need to understand the distinction between community service and Community service learning.

- Arranging community service learning logistics.

- Teachers need to have their theoretical knowledge clear and know the learning outcome thoroughly.

- The school teachers need to be trained to develop an understanding of essential elements of effective community service learning and design service-oriented activities based on the syllabus. It will enable them to gain knowledge and skill to implement community service learning.

- Teachers or community service learning coordinators need to take the children out to the neighbouring community to know the issues and to become aware of the community requirements which will help them to engage the children to develop the community service learning module based on the theory of different subjects that they study in the school.

- School administrators and teachers need to address the parents on the community service learning programme. They need to orient the parents on the complete process involved in executing the service activities with the community.

- School administrators/community service learning coordinators or the teachers need to meet the respective community head and orient them on it so that they can cooperate with the children.

4.7 Suggestions for the Teachers on Staying on the Right Track with Community Service Learning

Community service learning programme could be implemented for students from middle school to university.

- The administrators of the school need to understand the importance of community service learning as pedagogy.

- The result of community service learning will have more impact if it would have been for a longer period.

- Let the community and agency tell you about their needs.

- Get agreements from the respective stakeholders.

- Support the students in the preparation for the community service learning module and accompany them in executing it.

- Before and after the activities, the teachers need to conduct reflection.

- Parents could be invited to take part in the community service learning.

- Community agencies, NGOs, or other clubs could be invited to have partnerships with school children.

- The service activities could be pleasurable and physically and emotionally stressful activities should be avoided.

- It would be good to appoint a community service learning coordinator who can design the service activities and he/she could be a connecting person between the school, students, NGOs, and community.

Chapter 5

ASSESSMENT

Community service learning is experiential, revitalizing, and stimulating for the students, teachers, community, and school at large. It is very difficult to measure the behavioural and attitudinal changes. The following questions could be kept in mind while developing a community service learning module and implementing it.

- Whether regular community service learning is possible among high school students?

- Whether the modular approach is relevant for doing community service learning in the school?

- Is there any positive impact of community service learning among school children in developing their competencies?

- Is there any variation in the level of life skills on the basis of gender, religion, types of school, and family?

- Is there any attitudinal change that occurred among the parents of the school children who participated in community service learning and the teachers who teach them?

- Is there a significant difference in life skills of school children between pre and post-community service learning involvement?

- Is there a significant difference among school children based on age, the order in the family, religion, their place of residence (urban or rural), number of siblings, types of family?

- Is there a significance on children's life skills after the community service learning programme? Has it improved the civic values, civic responsibility, mother's and father's occupation, and study habits of school children?

The above questions will help to develop a standardized tool also to assess the impact of community service learning on life skills and competencies. There is a well-known Life Skills Assessment Scale that is used by many people who do research on life skills assessment.

5.1   Life Skills Assessment Scale

The Life Skills Assessment Scale (LSAS) developed by Dr. A. Radhakrishnan Nair, et.al (2010) was used for data collection. It is a standardized questionnaire having a reliability of 0.84 and a validity of 89%. The multi-dimensional life skills assessment scale consists of 100 items in the form of a statement, in-built with a 5-point scale for the respondent to check the appropriate response which is most descriptive of him/her. It has both positive and negative items. The scale measures 10 dimensions of life skills such as self-awareness, empathy, effective communication, interpersonal relationship, creative thinking, critical thinking, decision making and problem solving, coping with emotions, and coping with stress. This scale, as a whole, has split half reliability co-efficient by Cronbach alpha= 0.88, spearman-Brown coefficient =0.71 and Guttmann's split-half coefficient =0.71(p<0.001). Similarly, the concurrent validity of all scales ranges from 0.38-0.76 (p<0.001).

5.2 Survey Method for Personal Data (Annexure 3)

The personal data form is prepared in detail to collect socio-economic information from the students. This information helps to analyze and make a comparative study. Student's name, sex, age, order of birth, place of residence, qualifications, and occupation of the mother, qualification and occupation of the father, total annual income of the family, religion, caste, number of siblings and type of family

5.3 Checklist of Civic Value, Civic Responsibility, and Study Habit (Annexure 4)

A checklist containing 42 items could be used to assess if there are any differences in students' civic values, civic responsibility, and study habit by conducting the test before and after the community service learning intervention.

5.4 Interview

The teacher could use an interview schedule for collecting data from the principals of the schools. The objective of it is to understand their first response, when they heard about community service learning; what challenges they faced in making community service learning as a part of their school curriculum? What was their fear when children were taken to the community? More questions could help get the information from the management point of view of imparting life skills by involving school children in community service learning programmes.

5.5 Focus Group Discussion

A qualitative method of data collection can be used to assess the quality of community service learning intervention. Teachers, parents, and members of the community are the target population for the focus group discussion to assess their attitude towards the children who participated in community service learning programmes as they interacted with the children directly or indirectly.

The teacher could prepare a set of appropriate structured questions for each group separately. Then, the teacher could lead the discussion and prompt questions like what was their first reaction when their children were going out of the classroom to participate in community service learning programmes. What was their fear? Were they afraid that their classes would be hampered? Did they observe attitudinal change? More questions can be asked to motivate them to share their experience. The teacher could note down their responses during the discussion and a report can be prepared on the basis of the suggestions and observations of the participants. This discussion to be conducted in the schools only in the post-intervention stage.

5.6 Reflection Sheet (Annexure 5)

A reflection sheet is prepared for children to keep as a journal after they complete each activity. They could be encouraged to spend a few minutes in silence to gather all their experiences. The teacher needs to observe the children at every stage, during the preparatory session; during the preparatory discussion in the group, helping at the time of implementation of the activities, or guiding them to interact with the members of the community.

The school children will pen down their feedback in the reflection sheet and facilitate an open feedback session in the classroom. After every three activities, they are to be shuffled into a different group. This can be a challenging experience for them as they usually stick to their close friends. In the beginning, it will be very difficult for them to work with new friends in a new group but gradually they will appreciate and find it interesting when they get to know each other and make new friends. The technique of the reflection sheet will enable the teacher to guide the students and answer their queries especially when the students were emotionally disturbed.

5.7   Case Study

A case study is a descriptive and exploratory analysis of a person, group, or event. It is an in-depth investigation of a single individual, group, or event to explore the causes of underlying principles typically seen in social studies and life sciences. A case study of community service learning could be done to understand its efficacy and is considered as one of the best qualitative research methods.

Chapter 6

CONCLUSION

Education helps a child to convert information into knowledge. It helps to interpret experience into learning. True education is all about the lessons of life and this can be achieved only through experiential learning. Our education system needs to be oriented towards lessons with real-life situations. Education is not all about lessons from the textbook. Education needs to be Head, Heart and Hand (3H) based. It should stimulate the head to think critically and creatively. It should touch the heart of the learner and finally make a person understand the importance of doing or of an action using the hand. Such a 3H process is what makes any education complete. Most of the time, our present education system just stops at the cognitive level or may be one step behind the heart level. The most important aspect of psycho-social and psychomotor skills is neglected which actually strengthens the whole process of learning.

School is a mini society where children need to interact with their peers coming from all walks of life. The innovative interaction in the classroom prepares them to share their ideas and work in a team and collaborate. Community service learning gives them the opportunity to interact with and understand each other. It is important that children learn good things at an early stage of their life which will be engraved in their hearts. Community service learning helps to improve so many lives in the community as well as it enables one who is involved in the service of developing life skills. In this way, the giver also receives and the beneficiary too is helped.

In order to encourage, "learning to know, learning to be, learning to live together, and learning to do" among the present generation of children, life skills education needs to be imparted. There are many direct interventions that enable life skills among adolescents. It is proved that community service learning has made an impact on the overall life skills development among children. Such an experience does not just change one's life, it leaves an imprint in their lives because they will never be the same person, for as they come in touch with various learning experiences, it becomes their guidelines. Children build on what they already know and are provided with opportunities they make connections between new concepts and existing ones. Students have the chance to engage in the experience and practise what they have learned. It helps them in building strong relationships between feelings and thinking processes. Students have the capacity to learn successfully when the information is associated with values and feelings and community service learning is the best way to provide it to the students.

Adolescents are energetic individuals who learn best by doing, rather than talking. We need to adopt an unconventional and out-of-the-box thinking approach to promote life skills education. Therefore, community service learning would make use of a few school hours to conduct an intervention study with structured and planned activities in schools. It will result in some attitudinal change in children and help to build a positive outlook in day-to-day life.

Thus, engaging in community service learning would enable students, even at a young age, to realise that a deeper sense of fulfilment is gained from doing good work which goes beyond the satisfaction that is gained through achieving high marks, trophies, wealth and other material rewards. Community service helps the learners transcend themselves and connect with the larger community. This sense of oneness will, in time, help the students take ownership of their own well-being and that of the environment. Thus, the activities that are suggested for an integrated approach to this subject will eventually lead to a spiritual awakening in the student, leading to Maslow's ultimate objective of self-actualization.

COMMUNITY SERVICE LEARNING MODULE

Themes for 2 hours of activities

Sl. No	Area of Community Service Learning	Objective	Content	Process	Outcome	Time
1	**Education** Gender Equality	To develop self-awareness, coping with emotion, communication, and interpersonal relationships	**Theoretical Knowledge** Basic knowledge of gender Uniqueness of gender **Skill** To be able to differentiate gender **Attitude** All are the same and are equal **Value** Develop respect for human rights and dignity **Practical Action** Enact dramas and role plays.	Make students talk about their own families and their members. Evaluate how gender is being respected and valued. To enumerate the measures to be taken to respect gender. Describe the situations for the role plays. Select the characters for the role play and give instructions to the role players. Be prepared with the materials required to enact the drama/play. **Physical Activity Done:** Drama/role play was enacted. Explained to the local community the need to respect one's gender	Understanding of gender-related challenges. Enhancement of self-awareness, coping with emotions, teamwork, communication, and interpersonal relationship	2 hrs

| 2 | Awareness to open a savings account | To enhance communication skills, interpersonal relationships, decision-making, empathy, and self-awareness. | **Theoretical Knowledge**
Knowledge of micro-saving and its advantages.
Knowledge of different types of saving accounts

Skill
To be able to save and invest money

Attitude
Importance of saving money

Value
To enjoy a quality life

Practical Action
Helping people to open savings accounts | Prepare the children to make the local community aware of the importance of having a savings account.

Listing the names of the banks, information regarding the loan facilities, and the interest for the saving accounts at various banks.

Divide the students into groups and make them visit the families and make people aware of the savings account.

Physical Action Done

Spoke to the community members and helped them to open bank accounts | Learned about different types of banks, government saving schemes, and their benefits

Enhancement of Self-awareness, empathy, decision making, and problem solving. | 2 hrs |

Sl. No	Area of Community Service Learning	Objective	Content	Process	Outcome	Time
3	Each one teach one	To improve the skills of communication, empathy, interpersonal relationship, and problem-solving	**Theoretical knowledge** Children should have sound academic knowledge. Knowledge of different methods and techniques of teaching. Knowledge and awareness about the Child psychology of deprived children **Skill** Gain the confidence to teach **Attitude** Become helpful and caring **Value** Gain dignity, truthfulness, responsibility, and freedom **Practical Action** Prepared and learned the lessons to be taught. Prepare teaching aids, charts, flash carts, rhymes, and learn to conduct games.	After brainstorming, review the methods of teaching aids by adding some and deleting the ineffective ones. Explain to the students, the situation of deprived children due to poverty and first-generation learners. Listen to the suggestions and ideas that come from the students. Finalize the topics that need to be concentrated upon within the stipulated time. **Physical Action Done** Taught the lesson using the aids that were prepared by them. .	Learn English and numbers. Prepare class notes of primary level. How to handle children who are younger than them. Self-awareness, Empathy, creative thinking, critical thinking, and Interpersonal skills	2 hrs

| 4 | **Hygiene and Sanitation**

Hand washing techniques | To increase communication skills, self-awareness, and problem-solving | **Theoretical knowledge**
Knowledge of the importance and reasons for correct hand washing techniques.
Benefits of washing and keeping the hands clean.
Knowledge of diseases caused due to unclean hands.
Identify the critical times when they should wash their hands.

Skill
Ability to recognize when hands are dirty and need to be washed

Attitude
Positive attitude toward handwashing

Value
Keep clean and be safe

Practical Action
Supplying of soaps, hand wash liquids. Teaching various methods of hand washing. | Discuss issues related to diseases that spread by not keeping the hands clean.

Train and prepare the students for hand-washing techniques.

Students learn and practise in their groups.

Divide the students into groups of four or six to do the assigned project.

Physical Action Done

Distributed soaps and taught the techniques to wash hands.

Demonstrated the correct way of hand washing.

Communicated effectively to others the importance of hand washing. | Techniques of hand washing and the importance of hygiene and sanitation

Enhancement of communication skills self-awareness, creative thinking, and other social skills. | 2 hrs |

Sl. No	Area of Community Service Learning	Objective	Content	Process	Outcome	Time
5	Personal Hygiene	To improve self-awareness, interpersonal relationships, and communication skills	**Theoretical Knowledge** A good standard of hygiene prevents diseases, infections, and unpleasant odors which are important for mental health and quality of life. Good personal hygiene consists of bathing, washing hands, brushing teeth, and donning clean clothing. **Skill** The ability to keep themselves clean **Attitude** Body cleanliness is important. **Value** Self-care, respectful. **Practical Action** Demonstrating on how to keep oneself clean with the help of charts, posters, and video clips.	Brainstorming session on personal hygiene. Inviting the students to come up with the ideas and suggestions on this topic. Divide the students in to groups to prepare charts, posters and video clips. **Physical Action** Explained to the community the need for personal hygiene, its benefits, and importance.	Importance of good standard of personal hygiene which helps to prevent illnesses. Improvement in self-awareness, interpersonal relationships, and communication	2 hrs

| 6 | Safe use of toilets and urinals | To improve the skill of awareness, interpersonal relationships, and creative thinking | **Theoretical Knowledge**
To know the importance of safe usage of toilets and dirty urinals
Harmfulness of open defecation and urinals.
Practical tips to keep the toilets clean

Skill
Gain the ability to differentiate when the toilet is not clean and able to clean it

Attitude
They will begin to feel confident in themselves

Value
Preventing contamination of their environment.

Practical Action
Prepared charts explaining the diseases that spread through contaminated/unsafe toilets.
Demonstrated to the community the different methods to keep one's toilet clean | Discussion about how to keep the toilets clean and diseases caused through unsafe use of toilets.

Divide the students into small groups and prepare charts on the harmfulness of open defecation and urinals.

Learn to demonstrate to keep one's toilet clean.

Physical Action

Learned the importance of keeping toilets clean and become aware of the harmfulness of open defecation and urinals.

Prepared charts on diseases related to unsafe use of toilets and urinals.

Explained and demonstrated to the community the need for clean toilets. | Learn to keep the toilets clean and safe disposal of human urine and faeces to create a healthy life style.

Development of communication skills, self- awareness, interpersonal relations, and creative thinking. | 2 hrs |

Sl. No	Area of Community Service Learning	Objective	Content	Process	Outcome	Time
7	**Health** First Aid	To learn skills of communication and interpersonal relationship	**Theoretical Knowledge** To learn about the importance of using first aid. To know the requirements of different medicines in a first aid box Knowledge of the usage of each medicine Development of life saving skills **Attitude** Using of first aid box can prevent death **Value** Life is precious **Practical Action** Prepare first aid boxes out of shoe boxes. Collect different medicines in the box. Demonstrate how to use the medicine for a particular disease after identifying the symptoms	Discuss about the meaning of first aid, and the importance of giving first aid to save a life. Learn the names of the basic medicines which need to be collected to make a first aid box. **Physical Action done** How to use the medicines for different diseases. Collected the basic medicines to make first aid box. Demonstrated to people how to use the First Aid box	Learned about the meaning of first aid, and the importance of giving first aid to save a life. Learned how to use medicine for different diseases and lifesaving skills. Improvement visible in communication skills and interpersonal relationship	2 hrs

8	Balanced Diet	To learn to communicate, to become aware	**Theoretical Knowledge** To learn the balanced diet chart. Knowledge of proper nutrition for the human body to function correctly. Children with a poor diet run the risk of **growth, developmental problems,** and poor academic performance, and bad eating habits can persist for the rest of their lives. An unbalanced diet can cause diseases. **Skill** Eat healthy food. Able to listen to the body and eat accordingly **Attitude** Have a positive attitude towards food. **Value** What we eat matters. **Practical Action** Students were divided into groups to prepare the balanced diet charts for an awareness campaign. Conducted classes and discussions with the community members.	Discuss about healthy and unhealthy food Learn about the importance of a balanced diet. Prepare the chart of a balanced chart. To learn about the effects of an unbalanced diet. Divide into groups and prepare the balanced diet chart **Physical Action done** Explained to the people how important it is to eat healthy food and what diseases can be caused by unhealthy food. Conducted awareness campaign	Learnt the balanced diet chart and the specifications of vitamins, minerals, and nutrients to keep the body and mind strong and healthy. Enhanced the skill of effective communication, problem solving and interpersonal relationship	2 hrs

Sl. No	Area of Community Service Learning	Objective	Content	Process	Outcome	Time
9	Water- borne diseases	To learn the skill of communication, creative thinking and critical thinking.	**Theoretical Knowledge** List out water borne diseases. Identify ways in which water borne diseases are transmitted. State ways of preventing water -borne diseases. **Skill** Able to identify signs and symptoms of water-borne diseases. **Attitude** Water-borne diseases can be prevented by drinking safe water. **Value** Primary health care is wealth. **Practical Action** Learn all about water- borne diseases, its signs, symptoms and prevention measures. Prepared charts to communicate effectively the prevention of water-borne diseases.	Having a discussion on water-borne diseases and the signs and symptoms of each disease. Put them into groups and ask them to prepare charts, poems, songs and role play on the effect of water-borne diseases. **Physical Action** Communicated effectively the prevention of water-borne diseases.	Learnt all about water -borne diseases, their signs, symptoms and preventive measure. The skills of communication, creative thinking and critical thinking are improved.	2 hrs.

| 10 | **Environment**

Go Green March | To increase empathy for the earth and also to involve decision making and creative thinking | **Theoretical Knowledge**
Knowledge of the present environmental problems.
The effects of global warming: floods and drought
Global warming and the importance of go green

Skill
Able to organize a march

Attitude
Protect and preserve the environment

Value
Solidarity with the universe.

Practical Action
Prepare placards, banners, etc. | Explaining to the students the importance of going green and the consequence of not taking care of the mother earth.

Students will discuss the present situation of the environment and propose ideas regarding how to communicate to the local community around the vicinity of the school.

Students will also include the local community and well-wishers to join the march.

Distribute responsibilities for preparing the charts, posters etc.

Physical Action

Carried placards and banners and going for a march in a particular local vicinity. | Importance to conserve the environment

Empathy, decision making and creative thinking | 2 hrs. |

Sl. No	Area of Community Service Learning	Objective	Content	Process	Outcome	Time
11	Solid waste management	To improve the skills of decision making, critical thinking and communication skills	**Theoretical Knowledge** Name the refuse disposal practises in the local community Explain the significant correct and incorrect refuse disposal. Recycling means up -cycling which conserves energy, saves natural resources, reduces landfill **Skill** To distinguish the difference between degradable and non-degradable waste Identify the effective ways of disposing dry and wet refuse **Attitude** Small effort of waste management does make a difference **Value** Solid waste management saves the environment **Practical Action** Finding out the number of garbage disposal bins available. Getting the help of the municipality and providing sufficient garbage cans. Instruct the community to segregate different items into different cans.	Discuss the pitfalls of throwing the garbage on the road. Prepare the survey sheet to find out disposal practises and find out whether there are sufficient garbage cans in the local area. Talk to the people about the importance of good refuse disposal practises. **Physical Action** Surveyed to find out how many garbage cans are available. Communicated effectively how to segregate the waste. Demonstrated good refuse disposal practises and provided sufficient garbage cans.	Waste recycling helps to reduce the amount of fossil fuels and create a greener and cleaner environment for all. Improved in decision making, critical thinking, problem solving and communication skills.	2 hrs.

12	Plastic free life style	To grow in critical thinking, empathy and self-awareness	**Theoretical Knowledge** Awareness of the effects of plastics on the environment. Alternative means in place of plastics. Ways and means to get rid of plastic waste. **Skill** To identify different types of plastics. **Attitude** Challenge oneself to refuse, reduce, reuse, repurpose and recycle. **Value** Plastic free life can save the ocean. **Practical Action** Preparation of posters. charts, plays cards, etc. Explain to the people about the defects of using plastic bags.	Pose meaningful open-ended questions on environment. Discuss the causes due to the usage of plastic. Come out with ideas and suggestions regarding how to communicate it to the people. Divided the students into groups of six to execute the project. **Physical Action done** Explained to the local community the need to avoid using plastic bags. Students went around and collected the plastics and invited a recycling company and sold it.	Gained the knowledge on effect of plastics on the environment. Strengthen communication skills, self-awareness, decision making and problem solving	2 hrs.

Sl. No	Area of Community Service Learning	Objective	Content	Process	Outcome	Time
13	**Skill Development** Making of cloth bags	To improve creative thinking, communication skills and interpersonal relationship	**Theoretical Knowledge** The concept of recycling, knowledge of various house-hold things which could be made out of clothes. It could be used in place of plastic bags. **Skill** Able to make a cloth bag out of waste material. **Attitude** Environmental consciousness. **Value** All waste can be reused. **Practical Action** Collections of old clothes and other materials like scissors, thread, needles, etc.	State the need for skill development and ask the students for ideas. Giving training to the students. Putting them into groups and categorizing the items to be taught by them. **Physical Action** Students taught the community how to make cloth bags.	Importance of recycling and using cloth bags in place of plastic bags. Team work, Social responsibility, communicative skills, and empathy	2 hrs.

| 14 | Making of Paper Bags | To develop communication skills, and creative and critical thinking | **Theoretical Knowledge** Paper is re-usable and environment friendly and that it can be marketed. **Skill** Able to make a paper bag. **Attitude** Paper can reduce contamination. **Value** Paper is energy saver. **Practical Action** Children will learn how to make bags out of paper, in groups. They will teach the community how to make paper bags, its advantages, benefits, etc. | Discuss with the students how we can empower women and the local community, financially. Explain to them how paper bags are needed in the market and how they are eco-friendly. Students list out the requirements for making paper bags. Researcher/teacher trains students in making paper bags **Physical Action** They taught the community how to make different types of paper bags. | Students learnt team work, communication skills, creative and critical thinking | 2 hrs. |

Sl. No	Area of Community Service Learning	Objective	Content	Process	Outcome	Time
15	Making door mats	To improve creative thinking, communication skills, decision making	**Theoretical knowledge** To know the materials required to make door mats of different patterns and shapes. **Skill** Able to make a door mat. **Attitude** Door mat protects the dust from coming into the house. **Value** Door mats can be made out of waste. **Physical action** Collected old cloth, threads, etc.	Students learn how to make door mats. Prepared to take all the required materials to teach members in the community. **Physical action** Demonstrated how to make door mats.	Waste can be reused; saves energy and reduces pollution. Enhancement of creative thinking, communication skills and decision making	2 hrs.

Themes for 4 hours of activities

Sl. No	Area of CSL/ Activity	Objective	Content	Process	Outcome	Time
1	**Education** Survey to ensure zero drop outs	To develop interpersonal relationship, communication skills, empathy, self-awareness and creative thinking	**Theoretical Knowledge** Importance of knowing the context of the community. Information of the socio-economic condition. Detailed knowledge of the area selected. **Skill** To design a database to collect any information. **Attitude** To help and motivate those who dropped out of school. **Value** Grateful for the opportunity to be educated. **Practical Action** Preparation of the survey form. Visiting the family and filling in the survey form.	Discuss the situation of the drop-outs in the local area. Explain the importance of education. Putting the children into groups to visit the number of families in the local area. Instruction to the students on how to use the survey form. **Physical action** Met the families of the local area. The survey form is filled and the results are collated.	Important to know the issues and various problems faced by the community in sending their children to schools. Logical and critical thinking, social responsibility, interpersonal relationship, self-awareness and empathy	4 hrs.

Sl. No	Area of CSL/ Activity	Objective	Content	Process	Outcome	Time
2	**Health** Medical Camp	To improve problem solving, communication skills, interpersonal relations and decision making	**Theoretical Knowledge** Importance of health. Knowledge of different diseases. **Skill** Able to measure the height and weight of persons. **Attitude** Many people are in need of basic health care. **Value** Life is precious. **Practical Action** Necessary arrangement of things. Arrangement of the doctors, needed for the camp. Preparation of posters regarding the awareness of health issues.	Have an open discussion concerning health. Listen to students' opinions, ideas and suggestions. Designate a leader to record the ideas on the black board where everyone can see. Put them into groups and choose a leader for each group. Assign different duties to different groups. **Physical Action** Interacted with people Helped the doctors to record height and weight of the community members. Their health was checked/ monitored and made arrangements for medicines.	Importance of keeping good health. Learnt the names of different diseases and the prevention measures. Communicative skills, interpersonal relationships, Problem solving and decision making.	4 hrs.

| 3 | **Hygiene and Sanitation**

Shramdhan

Cleaning | To develop creative and critical thinking, decision making and problem solving. | **Theoretical knowledge**
Sense of Aesthetics.
Importance of cleanliness and environment protection.

Skill
Able to keep the surroundings clean.

Attitude
Cleanliness brings good health.

Value
Many hands make the work lighter.

Practical Action
Getting ready with the materials required such as brooms, sickles, garbage bags, masks, bleaching powder etc. | Discuss with the students, the situation of the unhygienic neighborhood.

Asking the students for suggestion.

Choose a leader to record all the suggestions and ideas.

After the brain- storming review, the ideas and add/delete and categorize them.

Put the students into groups and assign the work to be done.

Physical Action

Cleaned and beautified the unhygienic neighborhood. | Importance of cleanliness and clean environment, practised creative, critical thinking, decision making and problem solving | 4 hrs. |

Sl. No	Area of CSL/ Activity	Objective	Content	Process	Outcome	Time
4	**Environment** Plantation of saplings	To enhance critical thinking skills, communication skills, and decision making	**Theoretical knowledge** Awareness of ecology. How to take care of a plant. Knowledge of global warming. **Skill** Able to plant a sapling. **Attitude** Planting and taking care of saplings can save the universe. **Value** Trees are our partners. We need each other. **Practical Action** Collecting implements to make pits, collecting water, collection of saplings, etc.	Discuss the importance of planting trees. Explain to the students how to plant a sapling, what plant can be planted or will it thrive on a particular soil and in what season. Point out the areas for the planting. Divide the students into groups and assign them various responsibilities. **Physical action** Distributed the plants and taught the community how to nurture the plants.	Importance of planting sapling to prevent soil erosion and all the benefits of forestation. Communication skills, empathy and sense of social responsibility Learnt the reuse of the waste and reduce the landfills Developed the skill of creative thinking, problem solving and interpersonal relationship	4 hrs

5.	**Skill Development** Stitching of sarees together to make blankets with Kantha stitch	To learn the skills of creative thinking, critical thinking, problem solving and interpersonal relationship.	**Theoretical Knowledge** To know the importance of reusing old clothes. Knowledge of using needle and thread. **Skill** Knitting and sewing cloths. **Attitude** Don't throw away old clothes which can be used further. **Value** Maximum use of things available. **Practical Action** Collecting of sarees for making blankets, Students learn to stitch.	Get in to groups and they learn to put the sarees together and help each other stitch. **Physical Action** Taught the community to make blankets using sarees.	Learned to use old sarees otherwise thrown out. Enhanced creative and critical thinking skills, group work and teambuilding.	4 hrs

CONSENT FORM FROM PARENTS FOR PARTICIPATION OF THEIR CHILDREN

Dear Sir/Madam,

Community service learning is a fast-emerging subject of the 21st century. Many research papers have been conducted particularly about the usefulness and impact of community service learning and it is proved that it has a positive impact on the development of life skills and competency of school children. I request you to allow your child to participate in this study.

The participation involves being a part of a selected group of students to whom the community service learning intervention will be imparted by **(name of the teachers)** for the academic year —————- and will be done during school hours. Your child will be taken to serve the local community which is in close proximity to the school. All the service activities designed, will be based on their syllabus. This will be of great help for them as they will understand the theoretical concepts better. I/We will personally accompany them and take care of their safety. The involvement of your child will not, in any way, harm the child but it will help the child to become a better person and a better student. The aim of the study is to measure the enhancement of life skills through community service learning intervention. Your child's participation in this activity will be confidential. Only the concerned teachers will have access to the data collected. The analysis and discussion of the data will be presented in such a manner so as to ensure personal and institutional anonymity. You will be free to withdraw your child at any time from participating in the study. In case you have a concern about the study, you may contact me/us in the email id ——————————-

Please return this form with your signature indicating your consent for your child, to participate in this study. Only upon receiving the consent for your child, will you be contacted and he or she will become a part of life skills education group. Thank you for considering this request for your ward to participate in this research which will help the educated policymakers in creating a better tomorrow. I look forward to hearing from you, as per your convenience.

Sincerely,

Signature

________________________   ________________________

Signature of teacher   Signature of parent

Date:

PERSONAL INFORMATION

1. Name : (Please write your name in capital letters).

2. Gender : Male/ Female/3rd Gender

3. Age : 12/13/14/15

4. Religion : Hinduism/ Islam/ Christianity/ Buddhism/ Sikhism/ Jainism/ Any other

5. Residence : Rural/ Urban

6. Birth order : 1/2/3/4/other

7. No. of siblings : 0/1/2/3/3+

8. Father's Education : Illiterate/Primary/Secondary/ Higher Secondary/Graduate/ Post-Graduate/Professional

9. Mother's Education : Illiterate/Primary/Secondary/ Higher Secondary/Graduate/ Post-Graduate/Professional

10. Father's Occupation : Business/Private Employee/ Govt. Employee/No work

11. Mather's Occupation : Business/Private Employee/ Govt. Employee/No work

CHECKLIST OF CIVIC VALUE, CIVIC RESPONSIBILITY AND STUDY HABIT

Directions:

Read each statement carefully and respond truthfully:

Civic Value:

S. No	Items	Agree (2)	Disagree (1)	Not decided (0)
1.	Generosity makes you a better human person.			
2.	To work together in a group needs tolerance.			
3.	It is important to wait quietly in a queue, while booking your travel tickets.			
4.	When a responsibility is given, you are committed to your work.			
5.	To you, forgiveness builds relationship.			
6.	Patience helps you to make right decisions.			
7.	When you see the elderly standing in the bus, you unhesitatingly offer your seat.			

S. No	Items	Agree (2)	Disagree (1)	Not decided (0)
8.	Poor and vulnerable whom you see, need care and respect.			
9.	Every religion gives meaning to life.			
10.	You feel comfortable when you hear people speaking different languages.			
11.	Not to discriminate someone, on the basis of colour, is to be just.			
12.	Other person's beliefs and rituals needs to be respected.			
13.	Your loyalty to everyone in the family builds a happy home.			
14.	You dare to speak the truth even though you know that you would be punished.			
15.	Caring for the sick is an opportunity to serve.			

Civic Responsibility:

S. No	Items	Yes	No	Not sure
1.	Do you know the Preamble of the Indian Constitution?			
2.	Do you know the name of your City Mayor / President Grama Panchayat/ Municipal Chairperson?			
3.	Do you encourage your parents to vote in the elections?			
4.	When someone is denied justice, does it disturb you?			
5.	Can you raise your voice against discriminations?			
6.	Do you make an effort to save water?			

S. No	Items	Yes	No	Not sure
7.	Do you say "NO" to plastic bags when they are given to you?			
8.	Do you treat public property as your own?			
9.	Do you have the habit of reading newspaper and watching the news on TV daily, to stay abreast on current affairs?			
10.	Are you aware of the various schemes given by the government for the welfare of the people?			
11.	When you see waste lying on the floor, do you feel the need to pick it up and dispose of it in the dustbin?			
12.	Do you pay when you use public transport?			

Academic Skills:

S. No	Items	True	False	Not Aware/ Not applicable
1.	Learning takes place, every moment and everywhere.			
2.	I have the habit of being attentive in class.			
3.	Taking notes regularly helps me to study better.			
4.	I am comfortable, when I have discussions with my peers and teachers.			
5.	Borrowing books from the library and reading them is a regular practise for me.			
6.	Participating in seminars and conferences increases my learning.			

S. No	Items	True	False	Not Aware/ Not applicable
7.	I do my homework regularly.			
8.	I tend to bunk classes often.			
9.	Hard work helps me to score good marks.			
10.	I enjoy a cordial relationship with my teachers.			
11.	I prepare well ahead of time for my examination.			
12.	The fear of examinations bothers me very often.			
13.	I understand quickly when subjects are taught to me.			
14.	I can connect my lesson to situations of daily life.			
15.	I am able to balance my study and free time.			

REFLECTING ON COMMUNITY SERVICE LEARNING

INSTRUCTIONS: The Reflection Form should be completed by the student. Reflection happens before, during and after a student's service experience to encourage students to evaluate personal, social and civic issues related to their world and its connections to public policy and civic life. Please submit your reflection documentation to your community service learning Provider along with this form.

Name of the school:

Boy/ Girl:

Name of the school:

Date of the community service learning done:

Duration:

Name of the activity:

Venue and the target group:

1. What are the key points that you have learned in, and through the activities today?

2. Are you able to connect to or associate with anything that you study in your syllabus?

3. Please describe any moving experience, if any (joyful or any unpleasant):

4. How will you use the experience of this activity in your day-to-day life?

5. How did your service impact your school or community? How do you know?

6. How has your experience changed you as a person and challenged your earlier assumptions about people and social norms and structures?

LIST OF FIGURES

BIBLIOGRAPHY

Astin, A. W., Vogelgesang, L. J., Ikeda, E. K., & Yee, J. A. (2000). *How service-learning affects students*. University of California, LA: Higher Education Research Institute.

Astin, A.W., & Sax, L.J. (1998). How undergraduates are affected by service participation. Journal of College Student Development, Vol. 39(3), 251-263.

Balda, S & Sangwan, S. (2015). Competency building for management of aggression among Children. *International Journal of Life Skills Education*, Vol. 1(2), 57-74.

Bandura, A. (1977). *Social Learning Theory*. New York: General Learning Press.

Bettencourt, M. (2015). Supporting Student Learning Outcomes Through Service Learning. *Foreign Language Annals*, Vol. 48(3), 473-490.

Bharath, S., Kumar, K.V. (2008). Health Promotion using Life Skills Education Approach for Adolescents in Schools – Development of a Model. *Journal of Indian Association of Child & Adolescent Mental Health*, Vol. 4(1), 5-11. Bloomsbury, Great Britain.

Billing S.H. (2000). Research on K-12 school-based service-learning: the evidence builds. Phi Delta Kappan Vol. 81, 658–664

Bonnet, J (2008). *Engaging in Community Service and Citizenship: A Comparative Study of Undergraduate Students Based upon Community Service Participation Prior to College*. Thesis submitted to the Faculty of the Graduate school of the University of Maryland, College Park, in partial fulfillment of the requirements for the degree of Master of Arts.

Borden, A.W. (2007). The impact of service-learning on ethnocentrism in an intercultural communication course. *Journal of Experiential Education*, Vol. 30(2), 171-183.

Boss, J.A. (1994). The effect of community service work on the moral development of college ethics student. *Journal of Model Education*, Vol. 23, 183-198.

Braa, D & Callero, P. (20006). Critical Pedagogy and classroom Praxis. Teaching

Sociology, Vol. 34, 357-369. Keen, C & Hall, K. (2009). Engaging with difference matter: Longitudinal Student outcomes of Co-curricular Service-Learning Programs. The journal of Higher Education, Vol. 80(1), 59-79.

Bringle, R. G & Hatcher, J.A. (2000). Institutionalization of service-learning in higher education. *Journal of Higher Education*, Vol. 67(2), 273-290.

Brown M (2011) Learning from service: The effect of helping on helpers' social dominance orientation. *Journal of Applied Social Psychology*, Vol. 41(4): 850–71.

Buchert, L. (2014). Learning needs and life skills for youth: An Introduction. *International Review of Education*, Vol. 60(2), 163-176.

Camara, F. P. (2012). *The effect of Community Service on the Academic performance of Students at Massachusetts Middle School.* (Thesis submitted in partial fulfillment of the requirements for the degree of Doctor of Education, Northeastern University, Boston, Massachusetts).

Carson, R. L., & Domangue, E. A. (2012). Youth-centered service-learning: Exploring the professional implications for college students. *Journal of Community Engagement and Scholarship*, Vol. 3(2), 5-22.

Chambers, T. (2009). A continuum of approaches to service-learning within Canadian post-secondary education. *Canadian Journal of Higher Education*, Vol. 39(2), 77-100.

Celio, C. I., Durlak, J., & Dymnicki, A. (2011). A Meta-analysis of the impact of service – Learning on Students. Journal of experimental education, Vol. 34(2): 164-181.

Chessin, D., Moore, V. J., & Theobald, B. (2011). Exploring civic practices and service learning through school-wide recycling. *Social Studies the Young Learner*, Vol. 24(2), 23-27.

Chovance, D., Kanjner, T. A., Underwood, M (2012). Exploring shifts in conceptions of "good" citizenship: Community service-learning in activist placements. Cultural and Pedagogical Inquiry, Vol. 4(1), 43-56.

Chubbuck S. M (2007). Socially just Teaching and the Complementarity of Ignatian

Pedagogy and Critical Pedagogy. Christian Higher Education, 6, 239-265.

Coetzee, B. A., Bloemhoff, H. J., & Naude, L. (2011). Students' reflection on the attainment of competencies in a community service learning module in human movement sciences. *African Journal for Physical, Health Education, Recreation and Dance*, Vol. 17(3), 547-563.

Conrad, D., & Hedin, D. (1982). The impact of experiential education on adolescent development. *Child and Youth Services*, Vol. 4, 57–76.

Conway, J. M., Amel, E. L., & Gerwien, D. P. (2009). Teaching and learning in the social context: A meta-analysis of service learning's effects on academic, personal, social, and citizenship outcomes. *Teaching of Psychology*, Vol. 36, 233–245.

Csikszentmihalyi, M., & Schneider, B. (2000). *Becoming adult: How teenagers prepare for the world of work*. Basic Books: New York.

Daisy P.J., & Nair, R. (2018). An exploratory study on life skills intervention and its impact on the study skills among young adolescents. International Journal of Innovations in Engineering and Technology (IJIET).

Deans, T (1999). The Service –learning in two keys: Paulo Freire's critical pedagogy in the relation to John Dewey's pragmatism. *Michigan Journal of Community Service Learning*, Volume 6, Issue 1, 1999, pp 15-29

Deffenbacher, J., Lynch, R., Oettin, E., & Kemper, C. (1996). Anger reduction in early Adolescents, *Journal of Counseling Psychology*, Vol. 41(2), 149-157.

Delors, J. et al. (1996). *Learning the treasure within.* UNESCO, Paris.

Demir, Ö et.al., (2014) Validation and Reliability Study of Community Service Activities Scale in Turkey: A Social Evaluation. *Educational Research and Reviews*, Vol. X (XX), 456-465.

Dundar, H, Erdogan, E, Hareket. (2016). A role model in light of values: Mahatma Gandhi. *Educational Research Reviews*, Vol. 11(20), 1889-1895.

Einfeld, A., & Collins, D. (2008). The relationships between service learning, social justice, multicultural competence, and civic engagement. *Journal of College Student Development*, Vol. 49(2), 95-109.

Eyler, J. S. (2000). What do we need to know most about the impact of service-learning on student learning, *Michigan Community Service Learning*, 11-17.

Farahmandpour, H. (2011). *Beyond 40 hours: Meaningful community service and high school student volunteerism in Ontario.* (University of Toronto, Ontario Institute for studies in education)

Faure, E., et al (1972). *Learning to be. The world of education today and tomorrow*, Paris/London: UNESCO.

Fredericksen, P, J. (2000). Does service learning make a difference in student performance? *Journal of Experiential Education*, Vol. 23 (2), 64-74.

Giles, D.E., & Eyler, J. (1994). Theoretical roots of service-learning in John Dewey: Toward a theory of service learning. *Michigan Journal of Community Service Learning*, (1)1, 77-85.

Gogoi, A., Nathani, V., Manjukatoch. (2015). Life Skills Education for Healthy Living: A study among the Adolescents in Bihar. *International Journal of Life Skills Education*. Vol. 1(1): 44-52.

Goleman, D. (1997). Emotional Intelligence. Why it can matter more than IQ. Bloomsbury, Great Britain.

Gulhane, T.F. (2014). Life Skills Development through School Education. IOSR *Journal of Sports and Physical Education* (IOSR-JSPE), Vol. 1(6), 28-29.

Gutheil, I.A., Chernesky, R.H., & Sherratt, M.L. (2006). Influencing student attitudes toward older adults: Results of a service-learning collaboration. *Educational Gerontology*, Vol. 32(9), 771-784.

Hamilton, S. F., & Fenzel, L.M, (1988). The impact of volunteer experience on Adolescent Social Development: Evidence of program effects, *Journal of Adolescent Research*, 3(1), 65-80.

Hanson, W. (1992). *Prevention Programs: What are the critical factors that spell success?* Clemmons, North Carolina: Tangle wood Research Centre, Inc

Haynes, J. D., Sakai, K., Rees, G., Gilbert, S., Frith, C., & Passingham, R. E. (2007). Reading hidden intentions in the human brain. *Current Biology*, 17(4), 323-328.

He, Y., & Prater, K. (2014). Writing Together: Teacher Development through Community Service learning. Teachers and Teaching: Theory and Practice, Vol. 20(1), 32-44.

Hebert, A., & Hau, P. (2015). Student learning through service learning: Effects on academic development, civic responsibility, interpersonal skills and practical skills. Active Learning in Higher Education 16(1), 37-49.

Hedin, D. P. (1989). The Power of Community Service. *Proceedings of the Academy of Political Science,* 37(2), 201-213.

Hendricks, P. A. (1996). *Targeting life skills model.* Ames, IA: Iowa State University Extension.

Herzberg, B. (2006). Community Service and Critical Thinking. *College Composition and Communication*, Vol. 45(3), 307-319.

Hugg, R., & Wurdinger, S. (2007). A practical and progressive pedagogy for project-based service learning. *International Journal of Teaching and Learning in Higher Education,* Vol. 19(2), 191-204.

Jensen, S.V. (2006). Participation and Learning Relationships: A Service-Learning Case Study. *Journal of Industrial Teacher Education*, Vol. 43(3): 1-14.

Kackar-Cam, H., & Schmidt, J.A. (2014). Community-based Service-learning as a Context for Youth Autonomy, Competence, and Relatedness. *The High School Journal,* 83-104.

Kanjner, T., Chovanee, D., Underwood, M., & Milan, A. (2013). Critical community service learning: Combining critical classroom pedagogy with activist community placements. *Michigan Journal of Community Service Learning.* 36-48.

Kargar, F. R., Bita, A., Monir, K. G., & Shahnaz, N. (2013). Effect of Creative and Critical Thinking Skills Teaching on Identity Styles and General Health in Adolescents. *Procedia- Social and Behavioral Sciences*, Vol. 84, 464-469.

Kasinath H. M. (2013). Service Learning: Concept, Theory and Practice. *International Journal of Education and Psychological Research* (IJEPR), Vol. 2(2), 1-7.

Kaur, J., & Singh, D. (2015). Role of family in developing life skills and psychological hardiness among adolescents. *International Journal of Life Skills Education*, Vol. 1(1), 10-23.

Kay, K. (2009). Middle schools preparing young people for 21st century life and work. *Middle School Journal*, Vol. 40(5), 41-45.

Kendrick, J. R. (1996). Outcomes of service-learning in an introduction to sociology course. *Michigan Journal of Community Service Learning*, Vol. 3, 72-81.

Kiely, R. (2005). A transformative learning model for service learning: A longitudinal case. *Michigan Community Service Learning*, Vol. 12(1), 5-22.

Koh, K.C., et al. (2014). Role of Community Service as a Curriculum Delivery Tool in the Outcome-based Curriculum of the International Medical University. *IeJSME*, Vol. 8(1), 24-31.

Kolb, D. A. (1984). *Experiential learning: Experience as a source of learning and development*. Englewood Cliffs, N.J.: Prentice-Hall.

Kurian, A. (2015). The Extent of Life Skills among the Adolescents. *International Journal of Life Skilsl Education*, Vol. 1(1), 79-81.

LaGreca, A. M., & Santogrossi, D. A. (1980). Social Skills training with elementary school students: A behavioural group approach. *Journal of Consulting and Clinical Psychology*, Vol. 48, 220-227.

Larkin, R., & Mahoney, A. (2006). Empowering youth to change their world: Identifying key components of a community service program to promote positive development. *Journal of School Psychology*, Vol. 44, 513–531.

Lena, H. F. (1995). How can sociology contribute to integrating service learning into academic curricula? *American Sociologist*, Vol. 26(4), 107-117.

Lowery, D., May, D.L., Duchane, K. A., Coulter-Kern, R., Bryant, D., Morris, P. V., & Bellner, M. (2006). A logic model of service-learning: Tensions and issues for future considerations. *Michigan Journal of Community Service Learning*, Vol. 12(2), 47-60.

Mahmoudi, A & Moshayedi, G. (2012). Life Education for Secondary Education. *Life Science Journal.* Vol. 9(3), 1393-1396.

Mangrulkar, L., Whitman, C, V., & Posner, M. (2001). *Life skills approach to child and adolescent healthy human development.* D.C. Pan American Health Organization: Washington.

Markus, G. B., Howard, J. P., & King, D. C. (1993). Integrating community service and classroom instruction enhances learning: Results from an experiment. *Educational Evaluation and Policy Analysis*, Vol. 15, 410–419.

Masters, J. C., & Furman, W. (1981). Popularity, individual friendship selection, and specific peer interaction among children. *Developmental Psychology*, Vol. 17.

McAvoy, M. (2013). Training Faculty to Adopt the Ignatian Pedagogical Paradigm, IPP and its Influence on Teaching and Learning: Process and Outcomes. *Jesuit Education: A Journal,* Vol. 2(2), 62-109.

McDermott, J. J. (1981). *The philosophy of John Dewey. Volume I: The structure of experience. Volume II: The lived experience.* Chicago: The University of Chicago.

McDonnell, P. (2017). *The Experiential Library: Transforming Academic and Research Libraries through the Power of Experiential Learning.* Cambridge: Elsevier.

Meirose, C. E. Foundations. Washington DC: Jesuit Secondary Education Association, 2001.

Metcalf, L. E. (2010). Creating international community service learning experiences in a capstone marketing-projects course. *Journal of Marketing Education*, Vol. 32, 155-171.

Morgan, W., & Streb, M. (2001, March). Building citizenship: How student voice in service-learning develops civic values. *Social Science Quarterly*, Vol. 82, 155–169.

Nasheeda, A., Abdullah, H, B., Krauss, S, E., & Ahmed, N.B. (2019). A narrative systematic review of life skills education: effectiveness, research gaps and priorities. International Journal of Adolescence and Youth, Vol. 24 (3), 362-379.

Newman, B., & Newman, P. (1999). *Development through life. A psychological approach* (7th ed.), Wordsworth Publishing Co: Belmont.

Niemi, R.G et al. (2000). Community Service by High School Students: A cure for Civic Ills? *Political Behaviour*, 22(1), 45-69.

O'Keefe, J. M., (2015). Children and Community Service: Character Education in Action. *The Journal of Education*, Vol. 179(2), 47-62.

Oden, S. L., & Asher, S. R. (1977). Coaching children in social skills for friendship. *Child Development*, Vol. 48, 495-506.

Parida, P. (2015). A study on perception of communities of effectiveness Life Skills education (LSE) for promoting Adolescent reproductive & Sexual Health (ARSH) among tribes of Odisha. *International Journal of Life Skills Education*, Vol. 1(2), 75-81.

Parker-Gwin, R., & Mabry, J, B. (1996). Service Learning as Pedagogy and Civic Education: Comparing Outcomes for Three Models. American Sociological Association. Vol. 26(4).

Parmer, S., & Katoch, M. (2015). Promoting School Based Life Skills Education to Influence and Empower adolescents Towards Healthy Transition to Adulthood. *International Journal of Life Skills Education*, 1(1), 1-9.

Parvathy, V. & Pillai, R. (2015). Impact of life skills education on adolescents in rural school. *International Journal of Advanced Research*, Vol. 3(2), 788-794.

Perry, J. L., & Katula, M. C. (2001, July). Does service affect citizenship? *Administration and Society*, Vol. 33(3), 330–365.

Piaget, J (1972). *The Psychology of the child*, Basic Books Publishing: New York.

Powell, K., & Wells, M. (2010). The effectiveness of three experiential teaching approaches on student science learning fifth grade public school classrooms. *The Journal of Environmental Education*, Vol. 33(2), 33-38.

Prajapati, R., Sharma, B., & Sharma, D. (2017). Significance of Life Skills Education. *Contemporary Issues in Education Research* – First Quarter, Vol. 10(1).

Pujar, J. R., & Patil, S, S. (2016). Life skills development: educational empowerment of adolescent girls. *Research Analysis Journal of Applied Research*, Vol. 2(3), 551-565.

Radest, H. B. (1993). *Community service: Encounter with strangers*. Portsmouth, NH: Praeger Publishers.

Ramsaroop, S., & Ramdhani. R. (2014). A Critical Reflection of Service Learning: A Higher Education Perspective. *Mediterranean Journal of Social Sciences*. Vol. 5 (20).

Rani, R, & Menka. (2019). Life skills Education: concern for educationists for wholistic Development of Adolescents. *Paripex - Indian Journal of Research*, Vol. 8(1).

Ranjan, S., & Nair, R. A. (2015). Approaches and Strategies of Effective Implementation of life Skills Education. *International Journal of Life Skills Education*. Vol. 1(2), 89-110.

Reinders, H., & Yourniss, J. (2009). School-based required community service and civic development in adolescents. *Applied Developmental Science*, Vol. 10,12.

Rhodes, N.J., & Davis, J.M. (2001). Using service learning to get positive reactions in the library. *Computers in Libraries*, Vol. 21(1), 32-35.

Saleh, S. E. (2013). Paulo Freire's philosophy on contemporary education. University Bulletin, Vol. 15(l), 91-111. *Service Learning*, 15-19.

Shure, M. B., Spivack, G. (1980). Interpersonal problem solving as a mediator of behavioual adjustment in preschool and kindergarten children. *Journal of Applied Developmental Psychology*, Vol. (1), 29-43.

Simons, L., & Cleary, B. (2006). The influence of service learning on students' personal and social development. *College Teaching*, Vol. 54(4), 304-319.

Sivalingam, P., & Yunus, M. M. (2017). Nurturing 21st century skills through service learning: from isolation to connection. PEOPLE. International Journal of Social Science, Vol. 3(1), 346-356.

Skinner, R & Chapman, C. (1999). National Center for Education Statistic: A survey on Service-Learning and Community Service in K-12 Public schools.

Stetsenko, A. (2010). Teaching-learning and development as activist project of historical becoming: Expanding Vygotsky's approach to pedagogy. *Pedagogies: An International Journal*, Vol. 5(1), 6-16.

Strage, A. A. (2000). Service-learning: Enhancing student learning outcomes in a college-level lecture course. Michigan Journal of Community Service Learning, Vol. 7, 5-13.

Su, Yuling, & Chen K.H. (2014) Encountering Selves and Others: Finding Meaning in Life Through action and reflection on a social service learning. *Journal of Pacific RIM Psychology*, Vol. 8(2), 43-52.

Tatebe, J. (2013). Bridging gaps: Service learning teacher education: pastoral care in education, Vol. 31(3), 240-250.

Todd, S. (2008). Community Serving Learning: Introduction. *Canadian Association for social Work Education* (CASWE), Vol. 25(1), 87-88.

Usha Rao (2016). *Life Skills (Volume II)*. Himalaya Publishing House: New Delhi.

Vranda, M., & Rao, M. (2011). Life skills education for young adolescents and Indian experience. *Journal of the Indian Academy of Applied Psychology*, 37 (Special Issue), 9-15.

Vygotsky, L.S. (1978). *Mind in Society*. Cambridge, MA: Harvard University Press: Cambridge.

Warren, J. L. (2012). Does service-learning increase student learning? A meta- analysis. *Michigan Journal of Community Service Learning*, Vol. 18(2), 56-61.

Yates, M., & Youniss, J. (1996). *A Developmental Perspective on Community Service in Adolescence*. School K-12. Paper 38.

Yuen, M., Chan, R. M. C., Gysbers, N. C., Lau, P. S. Y., Lee, Q., Shea, P. M. K., Chung, Y. B. (2010). Enhancing life skills development: Chinese adolescents' perceptions. *Pastoral Care in Education*, Vol. 28(4), 295–310.